GLOBETROTTER TRAVEL ATLAS

Road Atlas of NAMIBIA

NEW HOLLAND

Published in 1994 by
New Holland (Publishers) Ltd
London • Cape Town • Sydney

ISBN 1 85368 519 4

New Holland (Publishers) Ltd
Chapel House, 24 Nutford Place,
London W1H 6DQ

Project Manager: Simon Atkinson
Text: Bill and Andrea Revilio
Editor: Sandie Vahl
Design Concept: Neville Poulter
Designer: Lyndall Hamilton
Cartographic Editor: John Hall
Cartographer: John Loubser
Cartographic Research: Estelle Cohen
Reproduction by Hirt & Carter (Pty) Ltd, Cape Town
Printed and Bound in Singapore by Tien Wah Press (Pte) Ltd

Photographic Credits
Gerald Cubitt: pages 6 left, 8 top left and top right, 11 top and bottom, 14 top and bottom right, 16 top left, 18 bottom left and bottom right, 20 bottom left and bottom right, 22 top right, 24 top right and bottom right, 26 bottom, 30 top right, 32 top right, 36 bottom left, 40 top left and top right, 42 bottom left, 44 top right and bottom left, 46 middle; **Roger de la Harpe:** page 8 bottom right; **Jean Du Plessis:** pages 6 top right and bottom right, 8 bottom left, 16 top right, 22 bottom left, 26 middle, 34 left, 38 middle left, 46 top right; **Willie and Sandra Olivier:** pages 14 bottom left, 18 top right, 20 top right, 22 top left, 30 middle left and right, 32 middle and bottom left, 34 bottom right, 38 top right and bottom right, 44 bottom right, 46 bottom left; **Peter Pickford:** cover, pages 30 bottom left [SIL], 34 top middle [SIL], 42 top left [SIL]; **Austin Stevens:** page 16 bottom right [PHOTO ACCESS]; **Peter Tarr:** page 24 bottom left [ABPL]; **Mark van Aardt:** title, pages 10 bottom, 11 middle, 42 top right; **Friedrich von Hörsten:** page 10 top; **Hein von Hörsten:** pages 26 top right; **Patrick Wagner:** page 28 [PHOTO ACCESS]

Distance Chart

ARANOS	AROAB	BETHANIE	GOBABIS	GROOTFONTEIN	KARASBURG	KARIBIB	KEETMANSHOOP	LÜDERITZ	MALTAHÖHE	MARIENTAL	OKAHANDJA	OMARURU	OSHIKANGO	OTAVI	OTJIWARONGO	OUTJO	REHOBOTH	SEEHEIM	SWAKOPMUND	TSUMEB	UPINGTON	VIOOLSDRIF	WALVIS BAY	WINDHOEK	APPROXIMATE DISTANCE IN KILOMETRES
	520	495	210	865	565	585	355	690	240	130	475	640	1150	775	655	725	318	400	800	835	825	655	830	405	ARANOS
520		300	870	1125	185	845	165	505	500	390	735	900	1410	1035	915	985	577	205	1060	1095	445	460	1090	665	AROAB
495	300		845	1100	345	820	135	265	220	365	705	875	1385	1005	890	960	551	95	1035	1070	605	435	1065	640	BETHANIE
210	870	845		660	915	380	705	1050	590	480	270	435	950	570	450	525	293	750	595	630	1175	1005	625	205	GOBABIS
865	1125	1100	660		1170	400	960	1300	845	735	390	345	375	90	210	280	547	1005	585	55	1430	1260	615	460	GROOTFONTEIN
565	185	345	915	1170		890	210	550	545	435	780	945	1460	1080	960	1030	624	255	1105	1140	260	190	1135	715	KARASBURG
585	845	820	380	400	890		880	1020	565	455	110	55	690	310	190	265	267	725	180	370	1150	980	210	180	KARIBIB
355	165	135	705	960	210	880		340	335	225	570	735	1250	870	750	820	414	45	895	930	470	300	925	505	KEETMANSHOOP
690	505	265	1050	1300	550	1020	340		375	565	910	1075	1590	1210	1090	1165	755	300	1235	1270	810	640	1265	845	LÜDERITZ
240	500	220	590	845	545	565	335	375		110	455	620	1135	755	635	705	299	380	780	815	805	635	810	390	MALTAHÖHE
130	390	365	480	735	435	455	225	565	110		345	510	1020	645	525	595	188	270	670	705	695	525	700	275	MARIENTAL
475	735	705	270	390	780	110	570	910	455	345		165	680	300	180	250	156	615	325	360	1040	870	355	65	OKAHANDJA
640	900	875	435	345	945	55	735	1075	620	510	165		635	255	135	210	322	780	235	315	1205	1035	265	235	OMARURU
1150	1410	1385	950	375	1460	690	1250	1590	1135	1020	680	635		380	495	570	834	1290	870	315	1720	1545	900	745	OSHIKANGO
775	1035	1005	570	90	1080	310	870	1210	755	645	300	255	380		120	190	455	910	490	60	1340	1170	520	365	OTAVI
655	915	890	450	210	960	190	750	1090	635	525	180	135	495	120		70	337	795	375	180	1220	1050	405	250	OTJIWARONGO
725	985	960	525	280	1030	265	820	1165	705	595	250	210	570	190	70		408	865	445	250	1290	1120	475	320	OUTJO
318	577	551	293	547	624	267	414	755	299	188	156	322	834	455	337	408		455	480	455	885	715	510	90	REHOBOTH
400	205	95	750	1005	255	725	45	300	380	270	615	780	1290	910	795	865	455		940	975	515	270	970	545	SEEHEIM
800	1060	1035	595	585	1105	180	895	1235	780	670	325	235	870	490	375	445	480	940		555	1365	1195	30	395	SWAKOPMUND
835	1095	1070	630	55	1140	370	930	1270	815	705	360	315	315	60	180	250	455	975	555		1400	1230	580	430	TSUMEB
825	445	605	1175	1430	260	1150	470	810	805	695	1040	1205	1720	1340	1220	1290	885	515	1365	1400		450	1225	975	UPINGTON
655	460	435	1005	1260	190	980	300	640	635	525	870	1035	1545	1170	1050	1120	715	270	1195	1230	450		1395	800	VIOOLSDRIF
830	1090	1065	625	615	1135	210	925	1265	810	700	355	265	900	520	405	475	510	970	30	580	1225	1395		425	WALVIS BAY
405	665	640	205	460	715	180	505	845	390	275	65	235	745	365	250	320	90	545	395	430	975	800	425		WINDHOEK

Town Plan Legend

Main roads & malls
Haupt und Einkaufsstraßen
Route principale et Mall
MALL

Roads
Straße
Route

Railways
Eisenbahn
Ligne de chemin de fer

Parks & sports fields
Parks und Sportplätze
Parc et terrain de sports

Route numbers
Routenummern
Numéros de routes
B4

Caravan parks
Wohnwagenpark
Camping pour caravanes

Hotels
Hotel
Hôtel
HANDKE H

Bus terminus
Endstation
Terminus bus

Buildings of interest
Wichtige Bauwerke
Monument à voir

Places of interest
Sehenswürdigkeiten
Endroit à voir
Tintenpalast

Hospitals
Krankenhaus
Hôpital

Places of worship
Gotteshaus
Lieu du culte

Police stations
Polizeirevier
Poste de police

Parking areas
Parkplatz
Parking

Post offices
Post
Bureau de poste

Library
Bibliothek
Bibliothèque

Information
Auskunftsbüro
Centre d'information

Built-up areas
Wohngebiet
Agglomération

One-way streets
Einbahnstraße
Rue à sens-unique

Major petrol stops
Große Tankstelle
Station-service

Contents

Key Tourist Areas

Main Map Section

The Namibian Flag was first raised when Sam Nujoma was inaugurated as Namibia's first democratically elected President on 20 March 1990.

National Route Planner

Key Tourist Areas

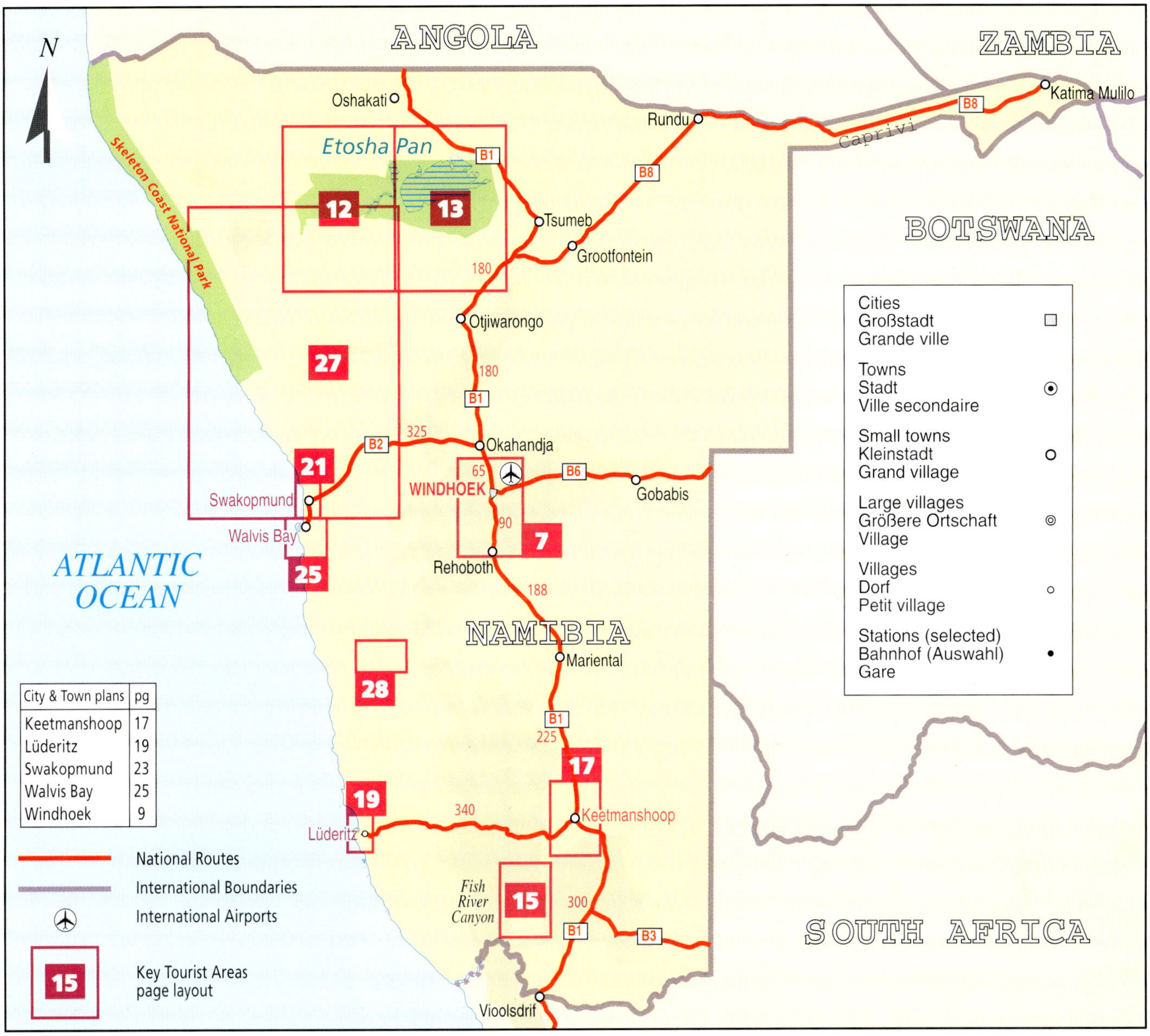

Legend

National roads Nationalrouten Route nationale		Railways Eisenbahn Chemin de fer		Airports Flughäfen Aéroports	INT. Other
Principal roads Nationalstraßen Route de liaison régionale		International boundary Internationalgrenze Frontière internationale		Places of interest Sehenswürdigkeiten Endroit à voir	Sesriem Canyon
Main roads Hauptstraßen Route principale	Tar Untar	Game & nature reserves Wild und Naturschutzgebiete Réserves naturelles	Etosha N.P.	Area names Gebiet Nom de la région	Damaraland
Minor roads Nebenstraßen Route secondaire	Tar Untar	Mountain ranges Gebirge Chaîne de montagnes	NAUKLUFT	Peaks in metres Höhe in Metern Sommet	Brandberg 2573m
Tracks Sandbahn Pistes		Scenic routes Malerische Landschaft Route panoramique		Water features Gewässer Hydrographie	River Pan Dam
Footpath Wanderwege Circuits de randonnées		Mountain passes Bergpässe Cols	Kuiseb	Major petrol stops Große Tankstelle Station-service	
Route numbers Routenummern Numéros de routes	B1 C36	Border posts Grenzübergang Poste de contrôle	Vioolsdrif	Hotels (selected) Hotel (Auswahl) Hôtel	H
Distances in kilometres Entfernungen in Kilometern Distance en kilometres	19 15			Camps Ferienlager Camp	

Windhoek Area

Namibia's capital city, Windhoek (see page 8), is sheltered by the Eros Mountains to the north, the Auas Mountains (Auasberge) to the south, and the rolling highlands of the Khomas Hochland to the west. On the popular Bosua route, one of the scenic drives through the Khomas Hochland, highlights include the Daan Viljoen Game Park, Liebig Haus and Von François Fort. Just east of Windhoek, the Avis Dam, though sometimes empty, is a good spot for bird-watching, especially just before the summer rains. The Goreangab Dam to the northwest of the city is a favoured venue for watersports such as windsurfing and yachting.

Visitors can enjoy game-viewing, from the comfort of a car or on foot, just 20km (12 miles) west of Windhoek in the Daan Viljoen Game Park, set among the rolling hills of the highland plateau called the Khomas Hochland. Gemsbok, eland, blue wildebeest, red hartebeest, Hartmann's mountain zebra, klipspringer and steenbok are some of the animals that can be spotted on the park's short circular drive and two self-guided walking trails, while bird-watchers can look out for rockrunner, white-tailed shrike and Monteiro's hornbill, some of the 260 bird species in the park.

Basic bungalows, overlooking the Augeigas Dam, offer accommodation for the budget traveller, and a restaurant serves meals three times a day. Day trippers should pack a lunch hamper and bathing costume as the park has picnic and camp-fire places and a swimming pool.

Daan Viljoen is on the road to Bosua Pass, the most northerly of the gravel-surface routes that lead from Windhoek west through the Khomas Hochland and then the Namib Desert to the coast.

The somewhat ramshackle Liebig Haus, about 50km (31 miles) from Windhoek along the pass, is a relic of Namibia's German colonial past. Built in 1912-13, it was probably a lavish country house in its heyday. About 14km (8.7 miles) farther on are the ruins of a fort built in 1890 by Major Curt von François to protect the route to the coast. It was later used as an outpost for German soldiers guilty of drunkenness, so it came to be known as *Trockenposten* or 'dry post'.

The tops of the Bosua, Us, Gamsberg and Spreetshoogte passes (about a day's drive from Windhoek and back) offer superb views of the undulating terrain of the Khomas Hochland that drops away to the expansive plains of the vast Namib Desert and the coast beyond, where the holiday town of Swakopmund is the main attraction.

Before you set off, it is always advisable to check on the condition of gravel-surface roads, especially after heavy rains.

WINDHOEK	J	F	M	A	M	J	J	A	S	O	N	D
AVERAGE TEMP. °F	74	73	70	66	61	55	55	61	66	72	72	75
AVERAGE TEMP. °C	24	23	21	19	16	13	13	16	19	22	22	24
Hours of Sun Daily	9	9	8	9	10	10	10	11	10	10	10	10
RAINFALL ins.	3	3	3	1.5	0	0	0	0	0	0.5	1	2
RAINFALL mm	78	77	79	38	7	1	1	1	3	11	27	42
Days of Rainfall	11	11	11	5	2	1	1	0	1	3	5	7

Left: *The gentle hills and valleys of Daan Viljoen Game Park, with the city of Windhoek and the Auas Mountains in the distance.*

Top: *Liebig Haus, a dilapidated two-storey mansion, features an indoor fountain and patterned tiles on the walls, and has a commanding view of the surrounding countryside.*

Above: *Augeigas Dam and the rest camp on its banks are a focal point at Daan Viljoen.*

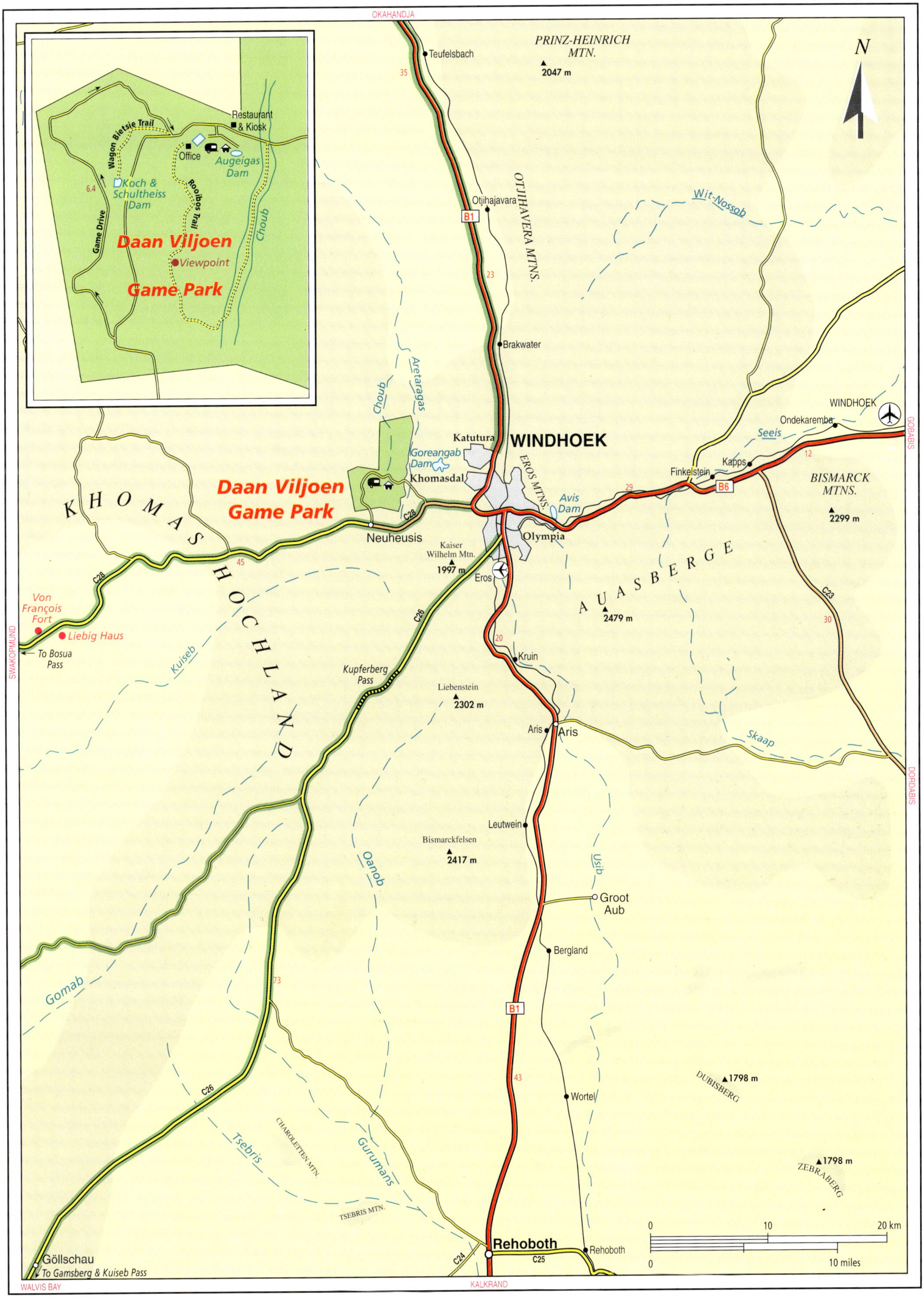
OKAHANDJA
Teufelsbach
PRINZ-HEINRICH MTN.
2047 m
N
Restaurant & Kiosk
Wagon Bietsie Trail
Office
Augeigas Dam
Koch & Schultheiss Dam
Rooibos Trail
Game Drive
Choub
Daan Viljoen
Viewpoint
Game Park
Otjihajavara
OTJIHAVERA MTNS.
Wit-Nossob
B1
Brakwater
Aretaragas
Choub
WINDHOEK
Ondekaremba
Seeis
Katutura
WINDHOEK
GOBABIS
Goreangab Dam
Khomasdal
Kapps
Finkelstein
B6
BISMARCK MTNS.
Daan Viljoen Game Park
EROS MTNS.
Avis Dam
2299 m
KHOMAS HOCHLAND
C28
Neuheusis
Olympia
Kaiser Wilhelm Mtn.
1997 m
Eros
AUASBERGE
Von François Fort
Liebig Haus
2479 m
C23
SWAKOPMUND
To Bosua Pass
Kuiseb
C26
Kruin
Kupferberg Pass
Liebenstein
2302 m
Aris
Aris
Skaap
DORDABIS
Leutwein
Bismarckfelsen
2417 m
Oanob
Usib
Groot Aub
Bergland
Gomab
B1
DUBISBERG
1798 m
C26
Wortel
Tsebris
CHARLOTTEN MTN.
Gurumans
1798 m
ZEBRABERG
TSEBRIS MTN.
C24
Rehoboth
Rehoboth
C25
0
10
20 km
0
10 miles
Göllschau
To Gamsberg & Kuiseb Pass
WALVIS BAY
KALKRAND

Windhoek City

Located among the undulating hills of the central highlands at a height of about 1650m (5400ft) is Namibia's capital, Windhoek, a lively, colourful mix of African and Western cultures. The climate here is relatively pleasant, although summer months are hot and frost does occur in midwinter. The city makes an ideal first stop for visitors to Namibia; not only does it offer an interesting variety of sightseeing attractions, a range of activities and good facilities, but from here a network of good roads leads to major attractions in other parts of the country.

Windhoek is a delightful mix of old and new, Europe and Africa – the colonial buildings in Independence Avenue would look quite at home in a German town, while colourful Herero women in traditional Victorian-style garb that is their trademark sell handmade dolls on the city's streets.

The city may be small (its population is only 160,000), but it has much to offer. If you want to learn more about Namibia's past and its people, visit the State Museum, housed in the Owela Museum Display Centre and the Alte Feste. The latter, an old German fort, is the oldest surviving building in the city.

Across the road from the Alte Feste, surrounded by well-kept lawns and shady trees, are the sandstone Christuskirche, built in 1910, with its tall steeple, and the Tintenpalast (1913), home of the Namibian Parliament. The Ombudsman's Office with its attractive brickwork and the turreted old school building are two more examples of German colonial architecture. The Warehouse Theatre, National Theatre of Namibia and Space Theatre offer culture and entertainment, and the Namibian Arts Association Gallery features a permanent display of local art.

Every first and second Saturday of the month Post Street Mall is a hive of activity as informal traders sell a variety of goods from basketry and woodcarvings to rag dolls and African jewellery. The Namibian Crafts Centre in Tal Street also sells handicrafts, while numerous art galleries, and shops that stock curios, gemstones, locally made jewellery, Swakara (karakul pelts) and leather goods, entice shoppers. A tea or lunch stop at one of the city's many cafés and restaurants is recommended.

Winter is a good time to amble along the Hofmeyer Walk, which runs along the ridge separating the city centre and Klein Windhoek, as the aloes are then in full bloom.

Above: *The clock tower at the top of Post Street Mall (bottom left) is a distinctive landmark in Independence Avenue, Windhoek's main thoroughfare.*
Above left: *Handicrafts on sale at the open-air market in Post Street Mall.*
Below left: *The Rider Memorial (1912) honours German soldiers killed in the 1903-7 Nama and Herero wars. To the right is the Christuskirche.*
Below: *Herero women in traditional dress.*

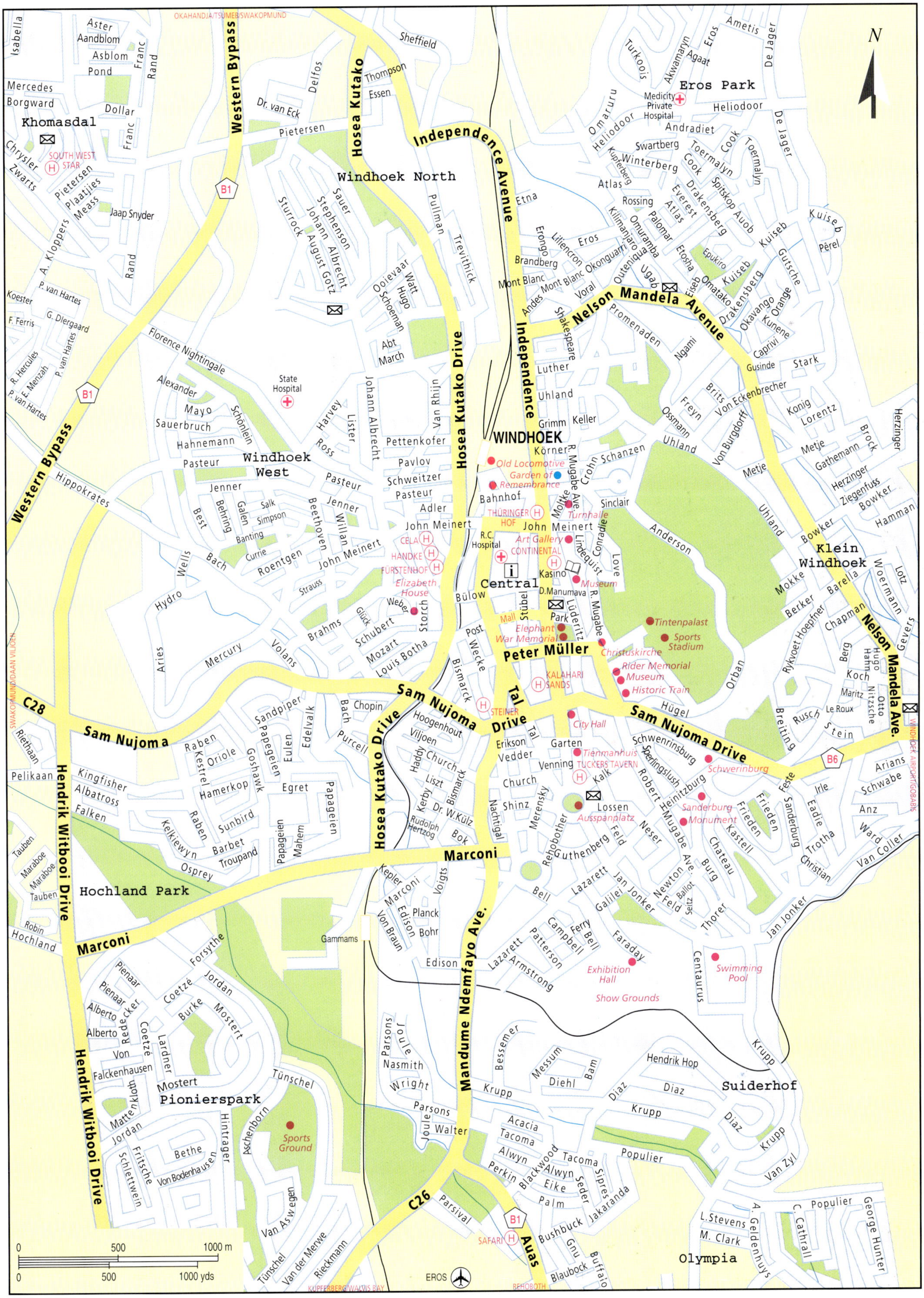
N
OKAHANDJA/TSUMEB/SWAKOPMUND
Khomasdal
Windhoek North
Eros Park
WINDHOEK
Windhoek West
Central
Klein Windhoek
Hochland Park
Pionierspark
Suiderhof
Olympia
Western Bypass
Hosea Kutako Drive
Independence Avenue
Nelson Mandela Avenue
Nelson Mandela Ave.
Sam Nujoma Drive
Sam Nujoma
Tal Drive
Peter Müller
Marconi
Mandume Ndemfayo Ave.
Hendrik Witbooi Drive
C28
C26
B1
B6
SOUTH WEST STAR
State Hospital
Medicity Private Hospital
R.C. Hospital
Old Locomotive
Garden of Remembrance
Turnhalle
Art Gallery
Museum
Kasino
Elephant War Memorial
Christuskirche
Tintenpalast
Sports Stadium
Rider Memorial Museum
Historic Train
City Hall
Tienmanhuis
TUCKERS TAVERN
Schwerinburg
Sanderburg
Monument
Lossen Ausspanplatz
Exhibition Hall
Show Grounds
Swimming Pool
Sports Ground
Elizabeth House
THÜRINGER HOF
CELA
HANDKE
FÜRSTENHOF
CONTINENTAL
KALAHARI SANDS
STEINER
SAFARI
Gammams
EROS
SWAKOPMUND/DAAN VILJOEN
WINDHOEK AIRPORT/GOBABIS
KUPFERBERG/WALVIS BAY
REHOBOTH
0 500 1000 m
0 500 1000 yds

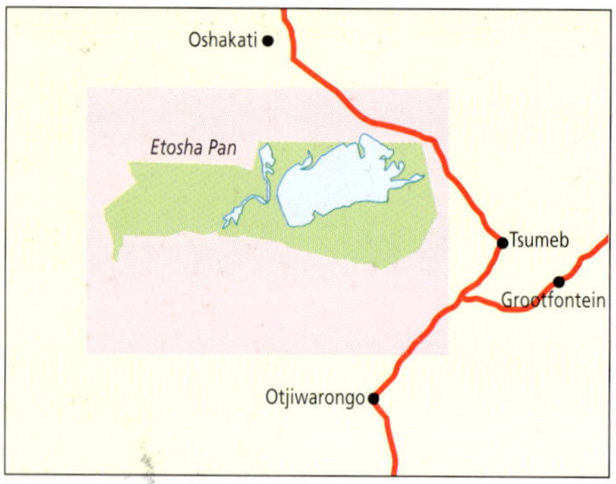

Etosha National Park

Known as the Great White Place because of its 5000km² (1930.5 sq miles) white clay pan that covers almost 25% of its surface, Etosha is one of the world's greatest game parks. Home to over 100 mammal species and a number of rare and endangered animals, this huge sanctuary stretches 300km (186 miles) from west to east and 110km (68 miles) from north to south at its widest point, and is 22,270km² (8598 sq miles) in extent. Although every day is a good day to spot a variety of wildlife at Etosha, the dry winter months, when animals congregate in the vicinity of waterholes, are the best time for game-viewing.

A trip to Namibia would not be complete without a visit to Etosha and an opportunity to spot the 'big five' – lion (easily spotted near waterholes in winter), elephant (reputedly the largest in Africa), leopard, buffalo and the endangered black rhino.

Hartmann's mountain zebra, roan antelope, black-faced impala and the diminutive Damara dik-dik are rare or endangered species that can be sighted. Giraffe, large herds of Burchell's zebra, springbok and gemsbok are common and cheetah, spotted hyena, warthog, ground squirrel, black-backed jackal (more likely to be seen in the early morning or late afternoon), eland, red hartebeest, common duiker and kudu are some of the other mammal species to look out for.

The 700km (435 miles) network of gravel-surface roads in the park that leads to the edge of the vast pan and the numerous waterholes give the visitor ample opportunities to spot up to 20 mammal species.

After good summer rains up to a million lesser and greater flamingos visit Fischer's Pan near Namutoni, along with a number of other migrant species from the north. Of the estimated 392 bird species in the park, bird-watchers should look out for Bradfield's swift, Rüppels parrot, and crowned crane on the Andoni Plains north of Namutoni, bare-cheeked babbler at Halali, and black-faced babbler in the eastern woodlands.

Much of Etosha is covered by mopane savanna and woodland, with dwarf shrub savanna on the fringes of the pan, grassland in the east and in a strip to the south of the pan, and pockets of tamboti and purple-pod woodlands and mixed tree and shrub savanna.

Of special interest, west of Okaukuejo, is the unique Moringa Forest, called the Ghost Forest or Haunted Forest because of the gnarled and grotesquely shaped trunks of the several hundred trees here (some trees even have two trunks). The moringa tree usually grows straight and upright and the eerily deformed shape of these specimens is thought to have been caused by browsing giraffe and elephant.

A historic fort is the focal point at Namutoni, a rest camp just 12km (7.5 miles) from Von Lindequist Gate, the entrance to the park in the east. Accommodation here ranges from rooms in the whitewashed, *beau gest*-style fort to caravan and camping sites, and a small museum depicts the turbulent military history of the outpost.

Farther west is Halali, at the foot of a small dolomite outcrop surrounded by mopane woodlands. Just 18km (11 miles) from the southern entrance, Andersson Gate, is Okaukuejo, the oldest rest camp and administrative headquarters of the park.

Accommodation at both Halali and Okaukuejo ranges from air-conditioned bungalows to caravan and camping sites. Facilities at all three rest camps include a restaurant, shop, swimming pool and filling station, and floodlit waterholes on the camp perimeters where you can put your feet up, sip a sundowner and wait for the night visitors – perhaps a slow-moving elephant, a majestic lion, or even a rhino. In addition, Okaukuejo features a limestone water tower which affords a superb view of the surrounding plains, and Halali has a short walk laid out on Tsumasa Hill.

Just outside the park, Mokuti Lodge, near Von Lindequist Gate in the east, and Ongava Lodge, close to Andersson Gate in the south, offer luxury accommodation and a variety of activities, including game-viewing drives and walks. Guided horse trails and a reptile park are attractions at Mokuti; Ongava Game Reserve has a small population of white rhino, and has both a luxury tented camp and wilderness camp.

Hobatere Lodge, situated in a 35,000ha (86,485 acres) game park that borders the southwestern corner of Etosha, is gateway to Damaraland (*see* page 26).

Accommodation at Hobatere is provided in en suite thatched-roof rondavels, and facilities include a swimming pool, *boma* and braai area, and campsite. Game-viewing day drives in the restricted western section of Etosha are conducted from the lodge.

ETOSHA PAN	J	F	M	A	M	J	J	A	S	O	N	D
AVERAGE TEMP. °F	79	77	75	73	66	61	61	66	73	79	79	79
AVERAGE TEMP. °C	26	25	24	23	19	16	16	19	23	26	26	26
Hours of Sun Daily	8	7	8	9	10	10	10	10	9	9	9	10
RAINFALL ins.	3	4	3	1	1	0	0	0	0	0	1	2.5
RAINFALL mm	75	109	75	26	18	1	0	0	2	7	31	68
Days of Rainfall	15	13	11	6	1	0	0	0	1	5	9	13

Opposite top: *A herd of springbok, accompanied by gemsbok and kudu, keep a wary lookout for predators near Okaukuejo.*
Opposite bottom: *The bizarrely shaped moringa trees of the Haunted Forest, west of Okaukuejo.*
Above: *Novel accommodation facilities are provided in the historic whitewashed fort at Namutoni rest camp. The original fort, constructed in 1903, has been rebuilt three times over the years.*
Left: *Guests observe a lone elephant on a game-viewing drive conducted from Hobatere Lodge.*
Below: *The world-famous waterhole at Okaukuejo offers visitors a theatre-style view of wild animals.*

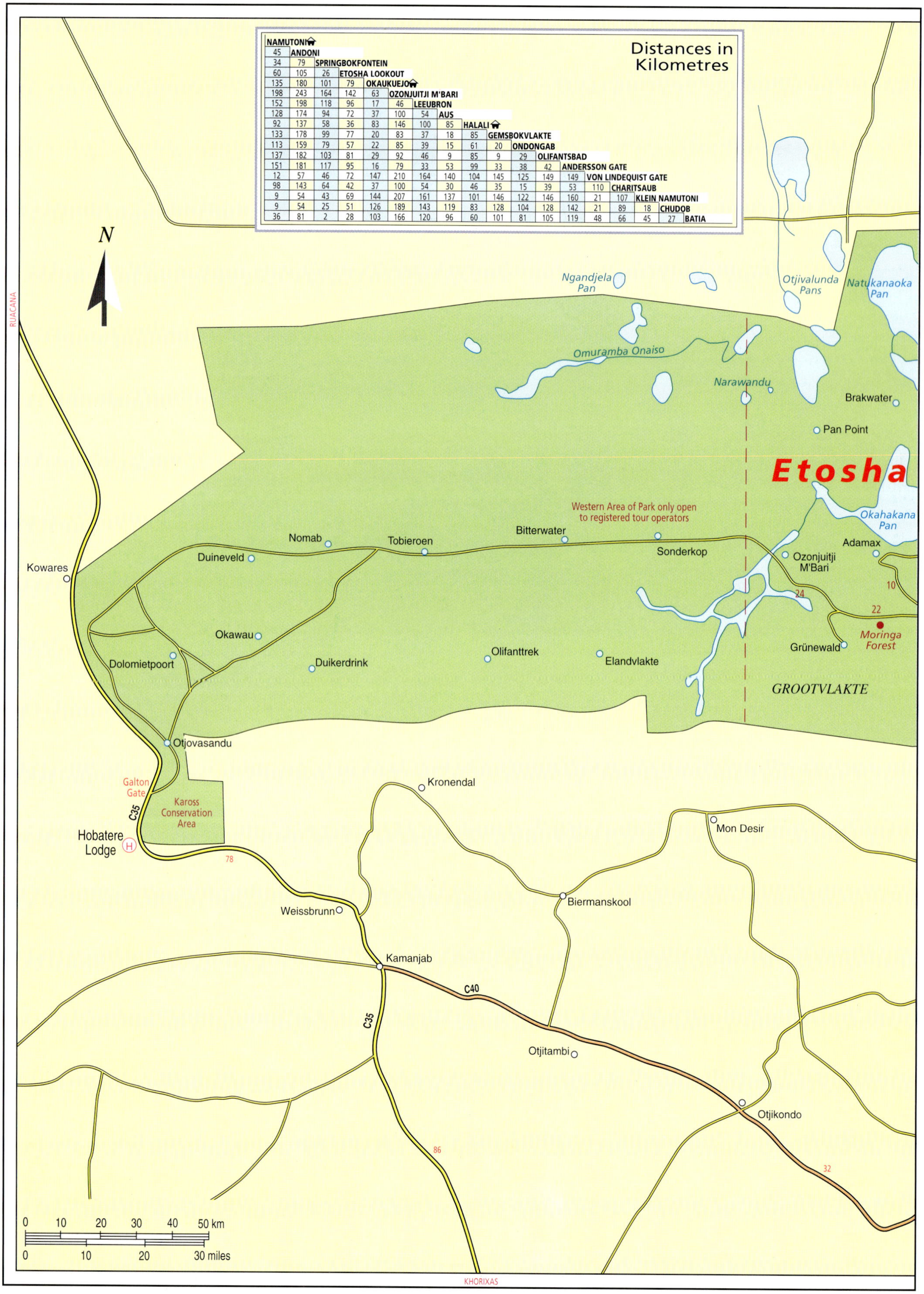

Distances in Kilometres

NAMUTONI																	
45	**ANDONI**																
34	79	**SPRINGBOKFONTEIN**															
60	105	26	**ETOSHA LOOKOUT**														
135	180	101	79	**OKAUKUEJO**													
198	243	164	142	63	**OZONJUITJI M'BARI**												
152	198	118	96	17	46	**LEEUBRON**											
128	174	94	72	37	100	54	**AUS**										
92	137	58	36	83	146	100	85	**HALALI**									
133	178	99	77	20	83	37	18	85	**GEMSBOKVLAKTE**								
113	159	79	57	22	85	39	15	61	20	**ONDONGAB**							
137	182	103	81	29	92	46	9	85	9	29	**OLIFANTSBAD**						
151	181	117	95	16	79	33	53	99	33	38	42	**ANDERSSON GATE**					
12	57	46	72	147	210	164	140	104	145	125	149	149	**VON LINDEQUIST GATE**				
98	143	64	42	37	100	54	30	46	35	15	39	53	110	**CHARITSAUB**			
9	54	43	69	144	207	161	137	101	146	122	146	160	21	107	**KLEIN NAMUTONI**		
9	54	25	51	126	189	143	119	83	128	104	128	142	21	89	18	**CHUDOB**	
36	81	2	28	103	166	120	96	60	101	81	105	119	48	66	45	27	**BATIA**

ONDANGWA
TSUMEB
OTAVI
OUTJO
OTJIWARONGO
Etosha Pan
National Park
Okasnanakana Pan
Olyapeke Pan
Gwishigambo
Ekuma
Poacher's Point
Logan's Island
ANDONI PLAINS
Andoni
Acacia
Mushara
Kameeldoring
Tsumcor
Aroe
Von Lindequist Gate
Fischer's Pan
Fort Namutoni
Groot Okevi
Klein Okevi
Namutoni
Etosha Aoba Lodge
Mokuti Lodge
Klein Namutoni
Okerfontein
Chudob
Kalkheuwel
Ngobib
Etosha Lookout
Springbokfontein
Nuamses
Goas
Batia
Noniams
Tsam
Halali
Rietfontein
Salvadora
Sueda
Charitsaub
Gonob
Homob
Okondeka
Wolfsnes
Leeubron
Ondongab
Kapupuhedi
Okaukuejo
Gemsbokvlakte
Aus
Olifantsbad
Dungariespomp
Gobaub
Ombika
Ongava Lodge
Andersson Gate
Toshari Inn
GOBAUBVLAKTE
Nuchas
Afguns
Uib
Goanab
Komukandi
Platveld
Marburg Mine
Nungubais
B1
C38
C39
C40

Fish River Canyon Conservation Area

Namibia's most spectacular geological feature is the magnificent Fish River Canyon, the second largest canyon in the world. Up to 549m (1800ft) deep and 27km (17 miles) wide, it has a total length of 160km (99 miles). The upper reaches of the rugged gorge were shaped by faulting of the earth's crust; the lower section was eroded by the gushing waters of the Fish River over millennia. Awe-inspiring vistas, a challenging backpack trail and hot springs are the drawcards that lure visitors to one of Namibia's prime attractions. A midsummer visit is inadvisable as temperatures soar to over 45°C (113°F) in the southern hinterland.

The most impressive part of the Fish River Canyon extends from just before the main viewpoint near Hobas, 65km (40 miles) southwards, and is best viewed when the sun is low in the sky as the changing pastel colours are at their most spectacular in the early morning and late afternoon.

Hobas campsite is about a 10-minute drive from the main viewpoint. Facilities are basic, but a grove of trees provides welcome shade and the swimming pool is a lifesaver on a hot day. The campsite is open all year round.

Ai-Ais, around 80km (50 miles) farther south, is only open from the second Friday in March to the end of October as the heat in summer is unbearable. Hot springs are the main attraction here, and facilities include an indoor thermal pool, a cooler outdoor pool, a range of accommodation from self-catering flats to camping and caravan sites, a shop, a restaurant and a filling station.

Bird-watchers will be interested in the more than 60 bird species recorded here, especially the scimitar-billed woodhoopoe, yellow-bellied eremomela and brubru.

Surrounding the greenery of Ai-Ais, and extending southward on the Fish River's journey to the Orange River on the Namibian-South African border, is a rugged landscape that is reminiscent of a stark lunar scene.

There is no better way to see the Fish River Canyon than by walking through it. Each year several thousand keen hikers tackle the 85km (53 miles) Fish River Canyon Backpacking Trail, which begins just north of the main viewpoint and ends at Ai-Ais.

The entire journey takes four to five days to complete and soft sand, boulders, temperatures of up to 40°C (104°F), the lack of facilities typical of a wilderness area and, sometimes, a shortage of fresh water make this a tough trail, but it is nonetheless very popular. The trail, is closed from the beginning of October to the end of April because of the excessive summer temperatures and the danger of flash floods in the canyon.

Below: *The mighty Orange River traverses a rugged and tranquil wilderness area (see page 46).*
Bottom: *The Fish River gently wends its way through the craggy splendour of the canyon it has helped to form.*
Below left: *Hikers negotiate the boulder-strewn river on the Fish River Canyon Backpacking Trail.*

FISH RIVER	J	F	M	A	M	J	J	A	S	O	N	D
AVERAGE TEMP. °F	68	68	66	64	63	61	59	59	59	63	64	66
AVERAGE TEMP. °C	20	20	19	18	17	16	15	15	15	17	18	19
Hours of Sun Daily	10	10	9	9	8	8	8	8	9	9	10	10
RAINFALL ins.	0	0	0	0	0	0.5	0	0	0	0	0	0
RAINFALL mm	1	3	2	4	4	9	5	7	3	5	1	2
Days of Rainfall	1	1	2	2	2	3	3	3	2	3	1	1

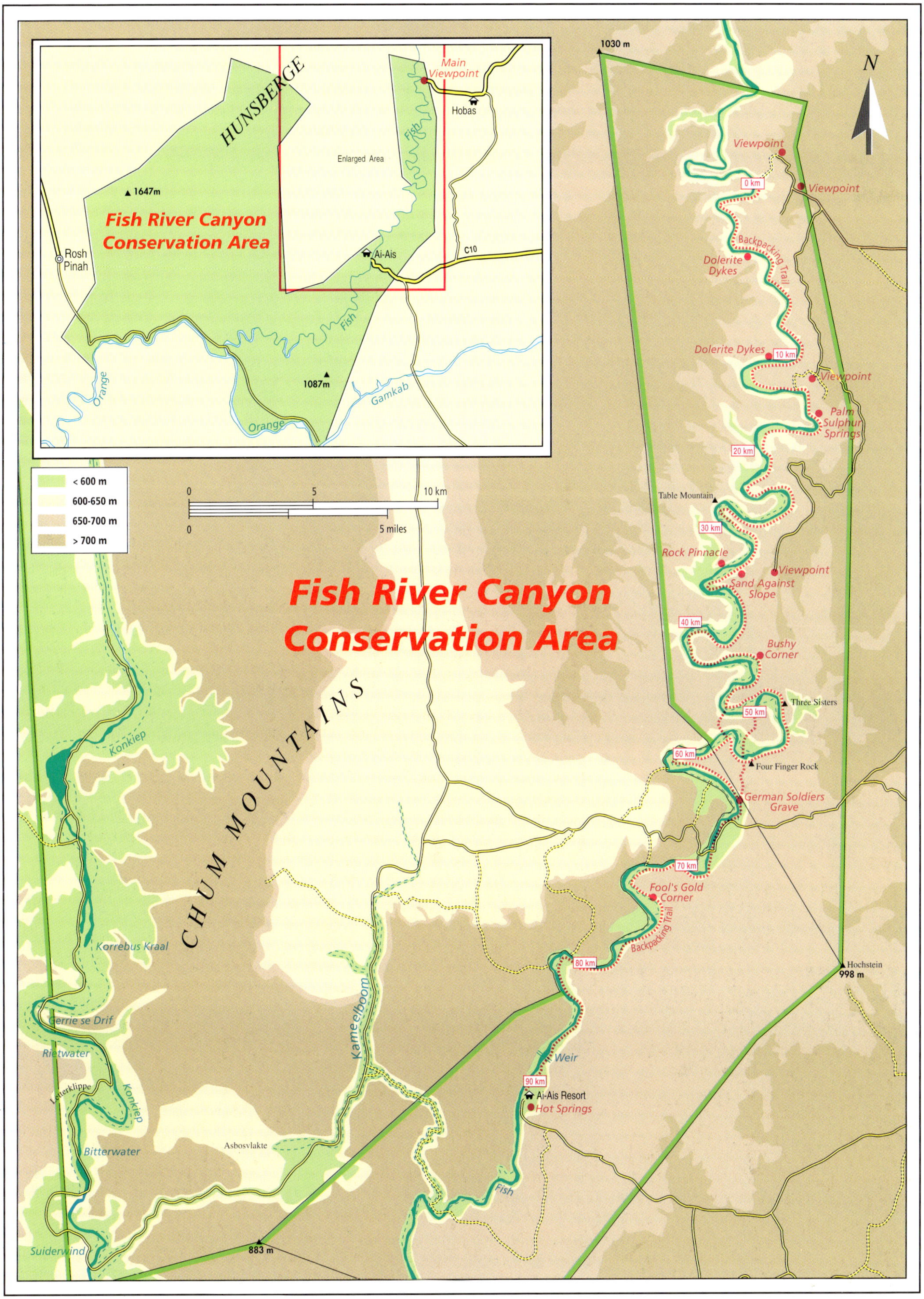

Fish River Canyon Conservation Area
HUNSBERGE
1647m
Fish River Canyon Conservation Area
Rosh Pinah
Enlarged Area
Main Viewpoint
Hobas
Fish
Ai-Ais
C10
Fish
1087m
Orange
Orange
Gamkab
< 600 m
600-650 m
650-700 m
> 700 m
0
5
10 km
0
5 miles
N
1030 m
Viewpoint
0 km
Viewpoint
Backpacking Trail
Dolerite Dykes
Dolerite Dykes
10 km
Viewpoint
Palm Sulphur Springs
20 km
Table Mountain
30 km
Rock Pinnacle
Viewpoint
Sand Against Slope
40 km
Bushy Corner
Three Sisters
50 km
60 km
Four Finger Rock
German Soldiers Grave
70 km
Fool's Gold Corner
Backpacking Trail
80 km
Hochstein
998 m
CHUM MOUNTAINS
Konkiep
Korrebus Kraal
Gerrie se Drif
Rietwater
Letterklippe
Konkiep
Bitterwater
Asbosvlakte
Kameelboom
Weir
90 km
Ai-Ais Resort
Hot Springs
Fish
Suiderwind
883 m

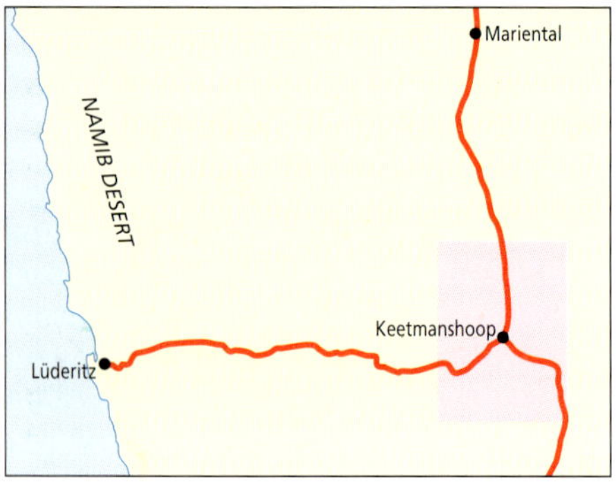

Keetmanshoop

About 500km (311 miles) south of Windhoek is the 'capital' of the southern hinterland and centre of Namibia's lucrative sheep-farming industry, Keetmanshoop. Here the Southern Tourist Forum actively promotes the many prime attractions of the south and provides up-to-date and comprehensive tourist information. Keetmanshoop is well placed for the tourist as national roads lead from here to Windhoek in the north, Vioolsdrif on the Namibian-South African border in the south and Lüderitz on the coast to the west, and an airport just outside the town is served by regular scheduled flights to and from Windhoek and Lüderitz.

Above: *Covered verandas were incorporated into German colonial buildings, like this attractive house in Keetmanshoop, to shield the core of the structure from the hot African sun.*
Left: *The historic tree-shaded town of Keetmanshoop is gateway to the many attractions of the southern hinterland (see pages 14 and 16).*
Below: *The distinctive silhouette of the drought-resistant quiver tree, or kokerboom, is a notable feature of the south (see page 46).*

The attractive Lutheran Church (1895) in Kaiser Street is testimony to the town's origins as a mission station. The historic building has been declared a national monument, and houses an interesting museum. Outside the church is a traditional Nama *matjiehuis* (a house made of thatched reed), while displays inside illustrate the history of the region.

The old hospital in Second Avenue, built in 1913 and called the Johanniterhaus, Schutzenhaus (1907) in Gibeoner Street, and the Old Post Office in the town centre, completed in 1910, are other historic buildings of interest. The latter has a distinctive broad rectangular tower, and serves as the offices of the Southern Tourist Forum.

Adventure-lovers and four-wheel-drive enthusiasts can obtain information about the Desert to Desert Trail at the Southern Tourist Forum. This seven-day self-guided expedition starts in the Kalahari Desert in the east and ends in the Namib Desert to the west, crossing a vast and remote area in between. Because the trail traverses such an isolated region, it is best to travel in a group of at least two vehicles.

Afrikaans-speaking people have named the countryside around Keetmanshoop *Vratteveld* as the outcrops of boulders strewn across the landscape look a bit like warts. The stacked stones are the remnants of dolerite which intruded into the overlying Karoo sediment and was subsequently shaped by weathering.

Karakul sheep are known as Namibia's black diamonds. Introduced in 1907 to the arid south, conditions these sheep are ideally suited to, karakul are a valuable source of foreign revenue as their pelts are exported world-wide to make fashion garments. Locally, their wool is used to weave rugs with creative and original designs. Black-headed Dorper sheep are also reared in this region, but for mutton.

KEETMANSHOOP	J	F	M	A	M	J	J	A	S	O	N	D
AVERAGE TEMP. °F	81	79	77	70	63	57	57	59	66	72	75	79
AVERAGE TEMP. °C	27	26	25	21	17	14	14	15	19	22	24	26
Hours of Sun Daily	12	10	10	10	10	9	10	10	10	11	11	12
RAINFALL ins.	1	1.5	1.5	0.5	0	0	0	0	0	0	0.5	0.5
RAINFALL mm	25	43	41	16	4	2	1	1	2	6	11	14
Days of Rainfall	11	11	11	5	2	1	1	0	1	3	5	7

MARIENTAL
To Kokerboom Forest
J.G.H. van der Wath
N
B1
C29
Aub
Golf Course
Noordhoek
Krönlein
C16
1023 m
Westdene
KEETMANSHOOP
Rifle Range
Kanonberg
994 m
Tseiblaagte
984 m
1041 m
B4
LÜDERITZ
Skaap
Gobas
Riverside
1016 m
0
2.5 km
1.5 miles
AIRPORT
2nd
14th
15th
16th Ave.
2nd Street
1st Street
Daan Viljoen
Kaiser
Conradie
TRAVEL INN
Schmiede
8th Ave.
6th Ave.
5th Ave.
Mittel
4th Ave.
3rd Ave.
2nd Ave.
1st Ave.
East
Fenschel
Jooste
11th Street
12th
22nd Ave.
Keetman Ave.
10th Street
Police Sta.
7th Ave.
Rhenish Church
Hendrik Nell
Luchtenstein
Aub
Westdene
23rd Ave.
24th Ave.
6th Ave.
Pastorie
Wheeler
CANYON
Ernst Kalweit
Diamond
Krag
Warmbad
Steen
River
5th Avenue
Tseiblaagte
Windhoek
Mimosa
Hostel
Klip
Suider
KARASBERG
300
300m
150
300 yds
Gold
Platina
Ferro
LÜDERITZ/GRÜNAU

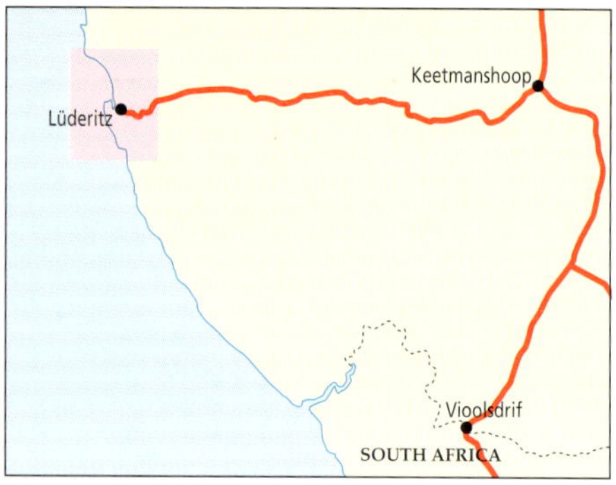

Lüderitz

Lüderitz is named after the man who set in motion the colonization of Namibia by the Germans, Adolf Lüderitz, a tobacco merchant from Bremen. It was at his request that Lüderitz Bay, which was then called Angra Pequena, and the surrounding area was declared a German Protectorate in 1884, 397 years after the first European, Bartolomeu Dias, sailed into the protected bay. Crayfishing is the major industry of this picturesque coastal town, which is surrounded by the diamond-rich Sperrgebiet (see page 44). Oyster cultivation takes place at Second Lagoon, while at Sturmvögel Bay there is the rusting remains of an old German whaling station.

Mist and windswept sand often cover the approach road to Lüderitz, a quaint coastal town that has retained its distinctive German atmosphere.

Colonial-style buildings of note in the town include Kreplin House (1909) with its asymmetrical façade, the Old Station Building (1914) and the houses in the Altstadt area. But it is on the slopes of Diamantberg (Diamond Mine) that you will find the two most impressive buildings. Goerke House (1910) is open to the public, and both the exterior architecture and interior decorative work are typically German. The Felsenkirche (1912) is open in the early evening, when the exquisite stained-glass windows are illuminated.

Also worth a visit are the Lüderitz Museum in Dias Street, the tourist-information centre, the Lüderitzbucht Foundation in Bismarck Street, and the Uugongo Art Centre where locally woven carpets and rugs reflect the beauty of the Namib Desert in their unique designs. Sandroses (or desert roses) – crystals of gypsum and calcium sulphate salts – are a favourite purchase at curio shops in Lüderitz. Visitors can dig for their own; however, a permit is required and one must be accompanied by an official.

Dias Point with its limestone cross (erected in 1488), wooden bridge (1911) and lighthouse (1910) is a highlight on a tour of the numerous enchanting bays of the Lüderitz Peninsula. Those who don't mind cold water can swim or surf at the long sandy Agate Beach, north of the town. Closer to town is Shark Island, connected to the mainland by a causeway, site of an often windswept campsite with a superb view and a plaque that commemorates Adolf Lüderitz.

The gaff-rigged schooner, *Sedina*, sets sail every morning, and, on calm days, continues to Halifax Island, home to a colony of jackass penguins. Passengers can view the penguins from the yacht, while on land these seabirds are best viewed through binoculars from the cliffs at Guano Bay.

A visit to Kolmanskop, a ghost town 9km (5.5 miles) east of Lüderitz, is highly recommended (*see* page 44).

LÜDERITZ BAY	J	F	M	A	M	J	J	A	S	O	N	D
AVERAGE TEMP. °F	64	64	64	63	61	59	57	57	57	59	61	63
AVERAGE TEMP. °C	18	18	18	17	16	15	14	14	14	15	16	17
Hours of Sun Daily	7	6	7	7	8	8	8	7	6	7	7	7
SEA TEMP. °F	68	66	64	63	63	59	59	59	59	59	61	61
SEA TEMP. °C	20	19	18	17	17	15	15	15	15	15	16	16
RAINFALL ins.	0	0	0	0	0	0	0	0	0	0	0	0
RAINFALL mm	1	1	2	2	2	3	2	2	1	1	1	1
Days of Rainfall	1	1	1	1	1	1	0	1	1	0	1	0

Above: *A unique sundial is a striking feature of Goerke House, a prime example of the charming colonial architecture in Lüderitz.*
Below left: *The ruins of an old guano station on Plumpudding Island, south of Lüderitz, has been colonized by jackass penguins.*
Below: *An aerial view of the town and harbour.*

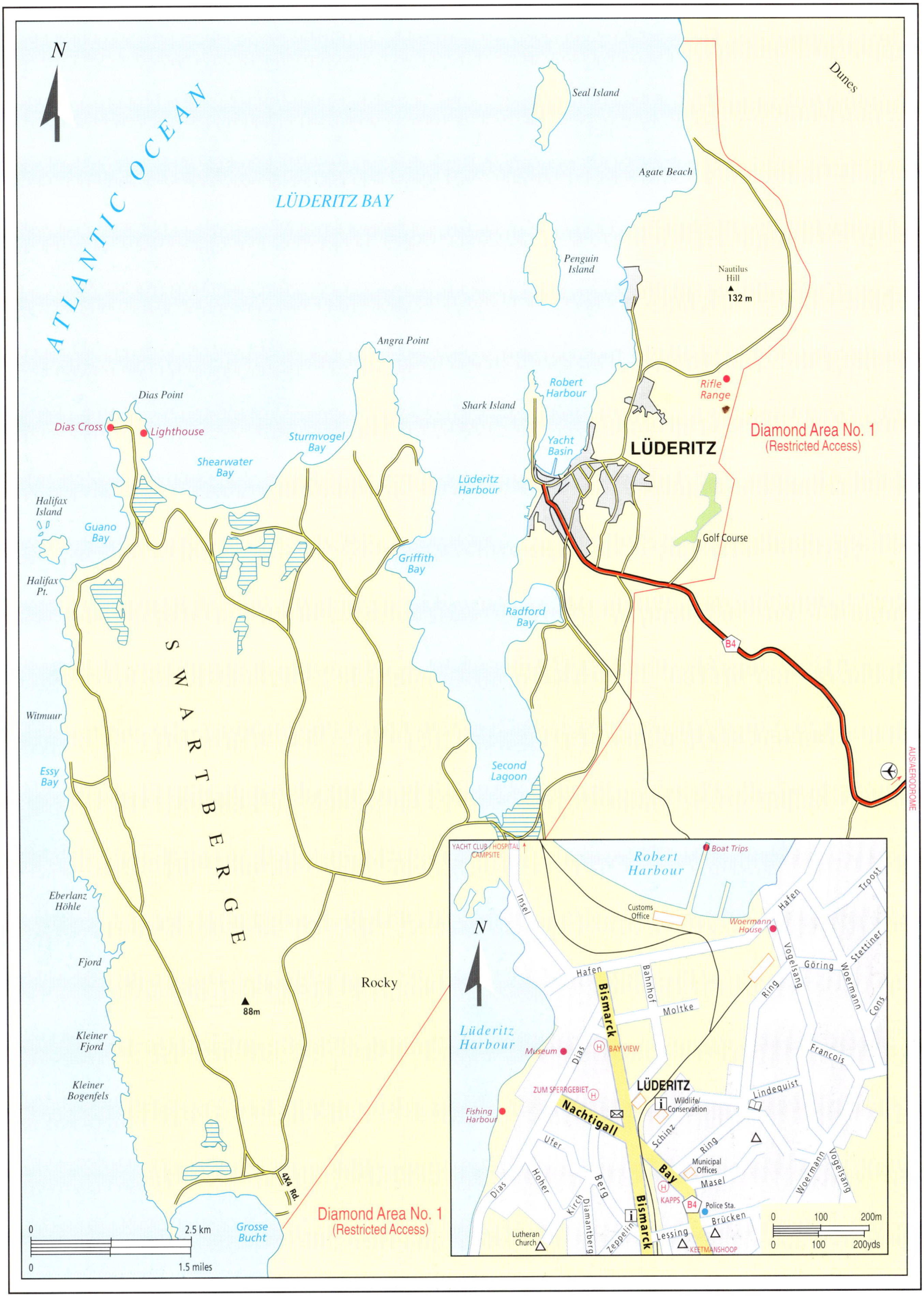
N
ATLANTIC OCEAN
LÜDERITZ BAY
Seal Island
Dunes
Agate Beach
Penguin Island
Nautilus Hill
132 m
Angra Point
Dias Point
Dias Cross
Lighthouse
Sturmvogel Bay
Shearwater Bay
Shark Island
Robert Harbour
Rifle Range
Yacht Basin
LÜDERITZ
Diamond Area No. 1
(Restricted Access)
Lüderitz Harbour
Halifax Island
Guano Bay
Griffith Bay
Golf Course
Halifax Pt.
Radford Bay
B4
SWARTBERGE
Witmuur
Essy Bay
Second Lagoon
AUS/AERODROME
Eberlanz Höhle
Fjord
Rocky
88m
Kleiner Fjord
Kleiner Bogenfels
4X4 Rd.
Grosse Bucht
Diamond Area No. 1
(Restricted Access)
0
2.5 km
0
1.5 miles
YACHT CLUB / HOSPITAL
CAMPSITE
Boat Trips
Robert Harbour
Insel
Customs Office
Woermann House
Hafen
Troost
N
Hafen
Bahnhof
Vogelsang
Göring
Stettiner
Bismarck
Moltke
Ring
Woermann
Cons
Lüderitz Harbour
Museum
Dias
BAY VIEW
Francois
ZUM SPERRGEBIET
LÜDERITZ
Wildlife/ Conservation
Lindequist
Fishing Harbour
Nachtigall
Schinz
Ufer
Ring
Municipal Offices
Bay
Woermann
Vogelsang
Hoher
Berg
Masel
Dias
KAPPS
B4
Police Sta.
Kirch
Diamantberg
Bismarck
Brücken
Zeppelin
Lessing
Lutheran Church
KEETMANSHOOP
0
100
200m
0
100
200yds

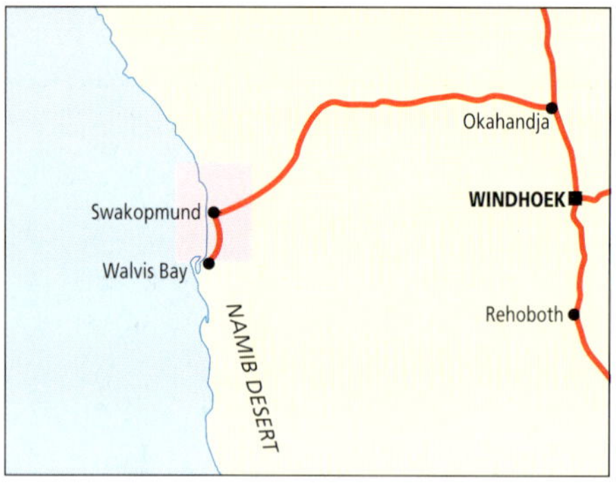

Swakopmund Area

The popular holiday resort of Swakopmund (see page 22) is a convenient base from which to explore the wonders of the Namib section of the Namib-Naukluft Park – all the main attractions in the 4,976,800ha (12,298,170 acres) park are accessible for ordinary cars, and facilities include a number of picnic places and basic campsites. The coast north and south of the town offers excellent angling conditions, while a camel farm, uranium mine and salt works provide interesting outings. Bird-watching is excellent along the coast, and, surprisingly, a number of mammal species have been recorded in the Namib Desert, including the beautiful gemsbok.

About 12km (7.5 miles) and 55km (34 miles) east of Swakopmund, are respectively, the Camel Farm and Rössing. The former offers the novelty of afternoon camel rides in the desert, the latter is the world's largest open-cast uranium mine, and may be visited by joining a tour that operates on Fridays. Northwest of Rössing are the salt works, and tours are offered here every weekday. Take along a pair of binoculars as the birdlife is prolific on the saltpans; flocks of lesser and greater flamingos are common.

The rich fishing grounds off the coast attract both fishermen and a variety of seabirds. Two resorts, Langstrand (Long Beach) and Dolfynpark (Dolphin Park), south of Swakopmund provide a range of facilities for anglers and holiday-makers. To the north is the popular National West Coast Recreation Tourist Area (*see* page 38), which boasts a number of basic campsites.

The 140km (87 miles) Welwitschia Drive, which starts about 20km (12 miles) from Swakopmund is the highlight of any visit to the vast gravel plains of the Namib-Naukluft Park. Features along the self-guided interpretive route are the geology, lichens and fascinating plants of the desert, the most notable plant being the giant *Welwitschia mirabilis* which is estimated to be about 2000 years old. This unique plant species is only found in the Namib, and the age of an average specimen is between 500 and 600 years. The lichen fields of the Namib are among the largest in the world (*see* page 38).

The scenery along the Swakop River Valley has appropriately been called the Moon Landscape as it is here that the river and its tributaries have cut deeply into the earth over millions of years, and subsequent erosion has added to the picture.

The spectacular Kuiseb Canyon (*see* page 40), apricot-coloured sand-dunes of Sossusvlei (*see* page 28) and rugged Naukluft Mountains (*see* page 40) are other highlights of the Namib-Naukluft Park.

Above: *Perhaps most well known of the desert-adapted plants of the Namib is the welwitschia. Only two ribbon-like leaves are produced, which tangle and tear in strong desert winds.*

Below left: *Sand-dunes meet the cold Atlantic Ocean along the barren coast of the central Namib Desert.*

Below: *A leisurely two-hour camel trek is an unusual way to explore the desert.*

SWAKOPMUND	J	F	M	A	M	J	J	A	S	O	N	D
AVERAGE TEMP. °F	63	64	63	60	60	59	55	55	55	57	60	63
AVERAGE TEMP. °C	17	18	17	16	16	15	13	13	13	14	15	17
Hours of Sun Daily	7	6	7	7	8	8	8	7	6	7	7	7
SEA TEMP. °F	68	66	64	63	63	59	59	59	59	59	61	61
SEA TEMP. °C	20	19	18	17	17	15	15	15	15	15	16	16
RAINFALL ins.	0	0	0	0	0	0	0	0	0	0	0	0
RAINFALL mm	1	1	7	1	0	3	0	0	0	0	0	0
Days of Rainfall	1	1	1	1	0	1	0	0	1	0	1	0

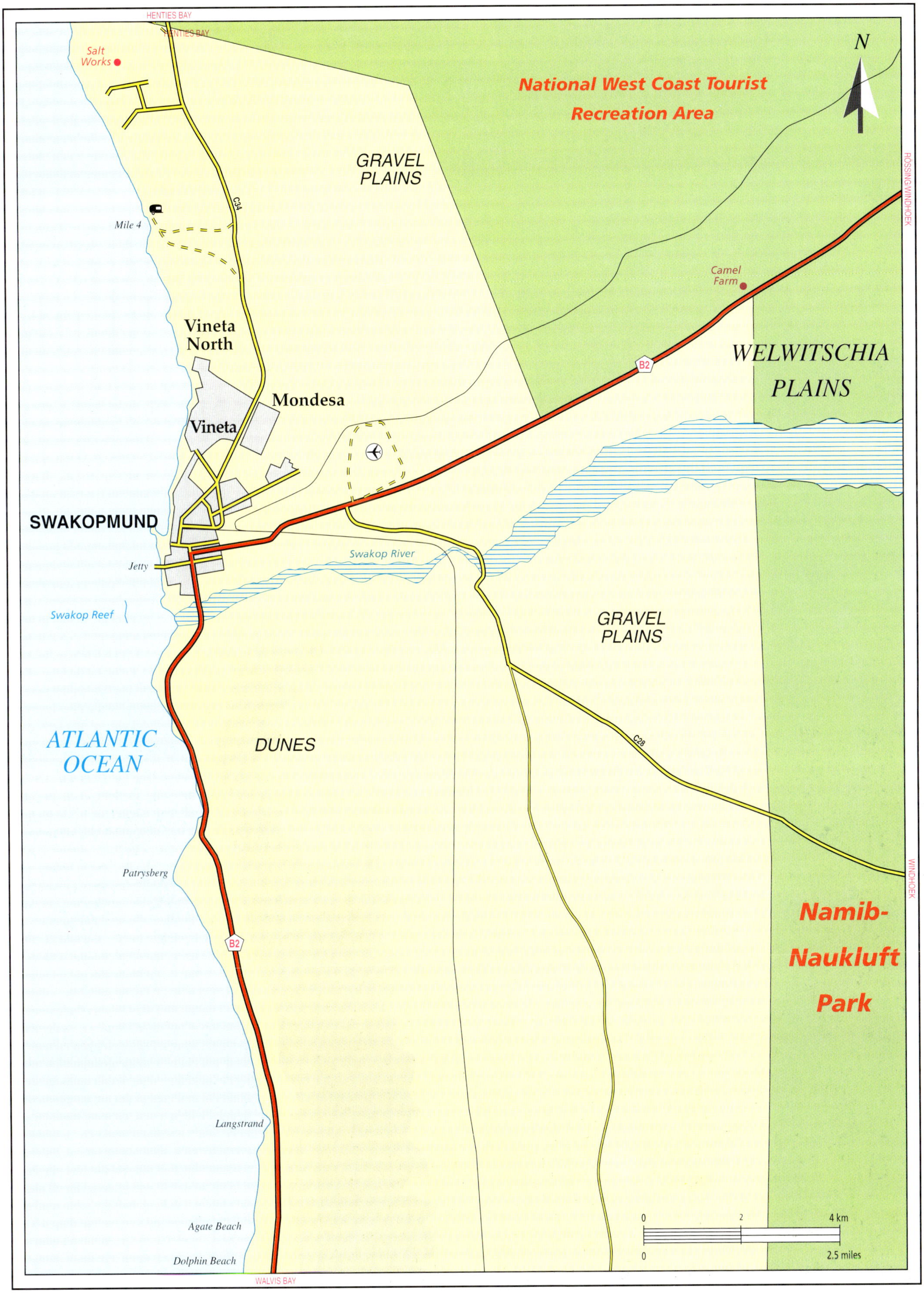
HENTIES BAY
Salt Works
N
National West Coast Tourist Recreation Area
GRAVEL PLAINS
C34
ROSSING/WINDHOEK
Mile 4
Camel Farm
Vineta North
B2
WELWITSCHIA PLAINS
Mondesa
Vineta
SWAKOPMUND
Swakop River
Jetty
Swakop Reef
GRAVEL PLAINS
ATLANTIC OCEAN
DUNES
C28
WINDHOEK
Patrysberg
Namib-Naukluft Park
B2
Langstrand
0
2
4 km
0
2.5 miles
Agate Beach
Dolphin Beach
WALVIS BAY

Swakopmund

Fog often blankets the 35km (22 miles) stretch of coastal road between Walvis Bay (see page 24) and Swakopmund, Namibia's premier holiday resort. There is much to attract the tourist in the beautiful town, and the moderate temperatures here are a relief after the unrelenting summer heat experienced in the interior. Swakopmund was founded in 1892 as a port for the inland German Protectorate that had been proclaimed in 1884, and the attractive German-style buildings are a tangible reminder of the town's colonial past, while German-speaking locals and a number of continental cafés and bakeries add to its individual character.

A stroll through the town is the best way to appreciate the beautiful German colonial-style buildings. There is the ornate, much-photographed railway station (1901) in Bahnhof Street, Woermannhaus (1905) in Bismarck Street, the lavishly decorated Hohenzollern-haus (1906) at the corner of Brücken and Moltke streets, which features a statue of Atlas, and the State House (1901-2), the President's official summer holiday residence.

Some other notable colonial buildings are Trendhaus in Molkte Street with its Bavarian-style window boxes, the elegant Villa Wille in Kaiser Wilhelm Street, and the huge fortress-like Alte Kaserne at the corner of Bismarck and Lazarett streets.

The Namib Publicity and Tourism Association is located in the elegant Woermannhaus, and provides tourist information on Swakopmund and the attractions of the Namib Desert, which surrounds the town on three sides. An art gallery on the premises exhibits local art, while the Damara Tower, originally built as a lookout post, is also part of the building and provides a great view of the town of Swakopmund.

The beachfront features a 262m (859.5ft) jetty, a lighthouse built in 1902, a swimming beach and a fascinating museum that contains ethnological displays, a collection of minerals and a reconstruction of the Adler Pharmacy.

Facilities at Palm Beach, where the water is actually too cold for more than a very quick swim, include a long waterslide and a heated swimming pool. Yachts and other pleasure boats are launched from the Mole, originally constructed, unsuccessfully, in 1899-90 to create a commercial harbour.

Shoppers will delight in the variety of goods on offer in the town – karakul rugs, hand-crafted leather goods, jewellery, local art, gemstones, ethnic artefacts and colonial-period antiques, and even first-day covers and stamps. Continental-style cafés offering a delicious selection of German confectionery invite one to stop for frequent coffee breaks.

Of interest along the approach road to Swakopmund, just before you reach the town, is an old steam engine known as *Martin Luther*. It was imported from Germany in 1896, came to a standstill shortly afterwards, and has not moved since.

Top: *Renovated and subdivided to serve as residential apartments in 1988, the beautiful Hohenzollernhaus is a superb example of baroque Wilhelmian-style architecture.*
Above left: *In 1910 another 10m (33ft) was added to the 11m (36ft) lighthouse constructed in 1902. In the foreground is the colonnaded State House, originally built to serve as a magistrate's court and formerly known as Kaiserliches Bezirksgericht.*
Left: *A leisurely stroll along the jetty is an ideal way to round off a day of sightseeing in Swakopmund.*

N
ATLANTIC OCEAN
HENTIES BAY
C34
Henties Bay Road
Turmalin
Aragonit
Karneol
Ruby
Saphir
Topaas
Dr. Schwietering
Fischreiner
Diamond
Aqua marine
Turmalin
Kormoran
Pelikan
Albatros
Flamingo
Agaat
Diamond
Opaal
Schwester Frieda
Seeadler
Diamond
Smaragd
Harder
Franke
Franke
Aldridge
Maritz
Omeg
Pinguin
Strandlopertjie
Kiebitz
Möwen
Fischreiner
Lumen
2nd Ave.
Möwen
Kühnast
Manta
Hoogenhout
Franke
Mossie
Mossie
Suikerbekkie
Uraan
Uraan
Cemetery
Kwikstertjie
Tin
Garnet
Copper
Tantalite
Mica
Granet
Silver
Kwarts
Goud
Platinum
Kwarts
Uraan
Vineta
First Ave.
Second Ave.
Hajo Brauer
Schluckwerder
Louis Botha
Riesle
Robert Blank
Roeder
Tamariskia
Graniet
Marmer
Dante
Dante
Plaath
Moseley
Sinden
Sports Field
Cemetery
Scultetus
Ugab
Makriel
2nd Ave.
First Ave.
Marine
Strand
Marshall
Boss
Dr. Welwitschia
Davies
Ocks
Haupt
Brockerhoff
Baumgarten
Ocks
Du Plessis
Meyer
Smith
10th Ave W.
11th St.
10th St.
8th Ave W.
9th St.
8th St.
9th Ave.
7th St.
6th St.
5th St.
10th Ave E.
4th St.
3rd St.
2nd St.
1st St.
8th Ave E.
6th Ave.
5th Ave.
12th St.
4th Ave.
3rd Ave.
2nd Ave.
10th
Mondesa
7th Ave.
1st Ave.
3rd St.
Woker
Central Sports Field
Sphinx
Woker
Richthofen
Dolphin
Richthofen
Nordring
Winter
Mondesa Sports Field
Schlachter
Kurze
Dunen
Welwitschia
Central Sports Field
Kolonnen
Phillip
Düsch
Strand
Kraal
Berg
Schlachter
Bäcker
Mittel
Knobloch
McHugh
Industry
Feld
Feld
Neser
Hafen
Werft
Heuschneider
Offen
Kraal
Kolonnen
Werft
Nordring
Schlachter
Schlosser
Koch
Garnison
Schlosser
SWAKOPMUND
WINDHOEK
Martin Luther Steam Tractor
B2
Mole
Swimming Bath
STRAND
Museum
State House
Strand
Police Station
Magistrates Office
Schul
Bahnhof
F. Stich
Wasserfall
DEUTCHES HAUS
Post
Francois
SCHWEIZERHAUS
HANSA
Estorff
Kaiser Wilhelm
Am Zoll
Omeg
ATLANTA
Rössing
Arandis
Trekkopje
Waterbank
Ebony
Aukas
RAPMUND
GRÜNER KRANZ
Lübbert
Leutwein
Nonidas
Namib
Kahn
Wildlife/Conservation
Woermann House
Woermann
Brücken
Südring
Lazarett
Kramersdorf
JAY JAYS
SCHÜTZE
Roon
Breite
Lüderitz
Windhuker
Scultetus House
Jetty
EUROPA HOF
Bismarck
Moltke
D'AVIGNON
Otavi
Cemetery
PRINZESSIN-RUPPRECHT-HEIM
Youth Hostel
B2
Rhode Allee
Unden
Cordes
Loopuyt
0
500 m
0
250
500 yds
Swakop
Strand
Swakop
GARNI ADLER
WALVIS BAY

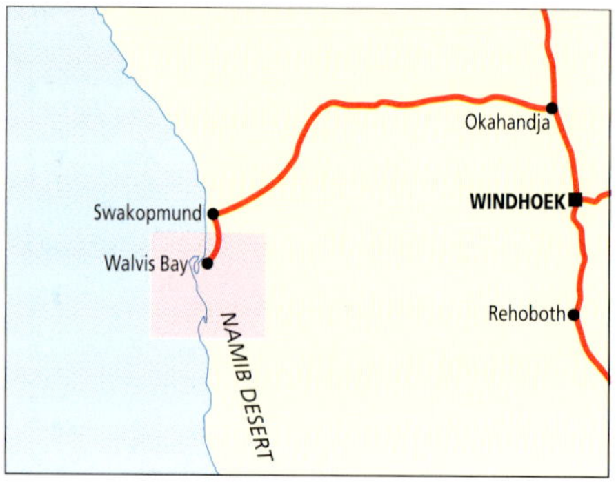

Walvis Bay Area

At midnight on 28 February 1994 the Walvis Bay enclave, a major commercial fishing port, and offshore islands were reintegrated into an independent Namibia after a long history of foreign powers staking their claim to the territory. Today watersports, angling and bird-watching attract visitors to the town. The lagoon is ideal for windsurfing and boating, while prime fishing spots are Paaltjies, 12km (7.5 miles) south, and several places along the coast between Walvis Bay and Swakopmund (see page 20). Bird-watchers can observe thousands of resident and migrant waterbirds in the Walvis Bay Nature Reserve and at Bird Paradise alongside Rooikop Road.

The fishing town of Walvis Bay lacks the quaint character of other well-known Namibian towns, but it is a mecca for bird-watchers. Thousands of lesser and greater flamingos can be seen on the lagoon, and the spectacular sight of the flock taking to the air is not to be missed. Greater flamingos are larger, white in colour and have a pink bill with a black tip; lesser flamingos are shaded pink and have a maroon bill.

The 45,000ha (111,197 acres) Walvis Bay Nature Reserve incorporates the lagoon, salt works (tours are conducted by request) and other intertidal areas as well as a section of desert. This important wetland area is a haven for up to 68,000 birds in winter and 80,000 in summer. Besides flamingos, other common species are the curlew sandpiper, sanderling and little stint; the chestnut-banded plover is a rare migrant species that can be spotted along the edges of the saltpans. Low tide is the best time for bird-watching, and the best way to appreciate what the reserve has to offer is to undertake a 3km (1.8 miles) walk along the Kuiseb River.

About 45km (30 miles) south of Walvis Bay is Sandwich Harbour, an unspoilt place of lagoon, sand-dunes and sea, and a sanctuary for a variety of birds. However, a four-wheel-drive is required to get to Sandwich, and most of the estimated 179,000 flamingos, pelicans, waders and terns are found south and west of the lagoon, in a 'no-vehicles' zone. Determined bird-watchers and explorers can undertake a 1.5- to 2-hour walk, and then walk back before nightfall as camping is not permitted.

Dune Seven, just east of Walvis Bay, is about 50m (163ft) high and a scramble to its crest will give you a bird's-eye view of the dune fields of the Namib.

Top: *The town of Walvis Bay, centre of Namibia's lucrative fishing industry.*
Right: *Sandwich Harbour, bounded by the Atlantic Ocean in the west and the sand-dunes of the Namib in the east, is a haven for migratory shorebirds.*
Far right: *Windswept sand often covers the highway that links Walvis Bay and Swakopmund, Namibia's premier holiday resort.*

WALVIS BAY	J	F	M	A	M	J	J	A	S	O	N	D
AVERAGE TEMP. °F	63	64	63	60	60	59	55	55	55	57	60	63
AVERAGE TEMP. °C	17	18	17	16	16	15	13	13	13	14	15	17
Hours of Sun Daily	7	6	7	7	8	8	8	7	6	7	7	7
SEA TEMP. °F	68	66	64	63	63	59	59	59	59	59	61	61
SEA TEMP. °C	20	19	18	17	17	15	15	15	15	15	16	16
RAINFALL ins.	0	0	0	0	0	0	0	0	0	0	0	0
RAINFALL mm	1	1	7	1	0	3	0	0	0	0	0	0
Days of Rainfall	1	1	1	1	0	1	0	0	1	0	1	0
Days of Mist/Fog	8	8	11	16	16	12	15	15	12	9	9	8

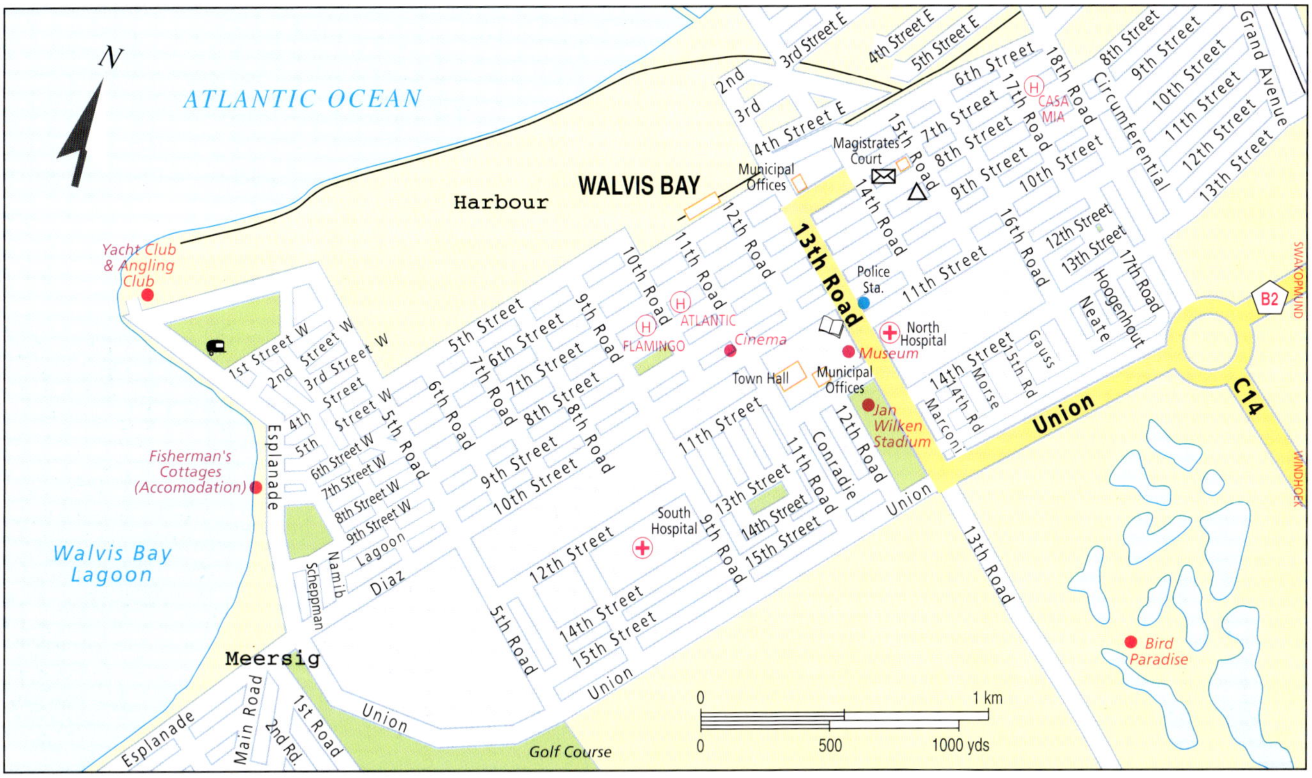

ATLANTIC OCEAN
Harbour
WALVIS BAY
Yacht Club & Angling Club
Fisherman's Cottages (Accomodation)
Walvis Bay Lagoon
Meersig
Esplanade
Main Road
2nd Rd.
1st Road
Union
Golf Course
Magistrates Court
Municipal Offices
Police Sta.
North Hospital
Museum
Cinema
Town Hall
Jan Wilken Stadium
South Hospital
ATLANTIC
FLAMINGO
CASA MIA
13th Road
Union
C14
B2
Bird Paradise
SWAKOPMUND
WINDHOEK
0
500
1000 yds
1 km

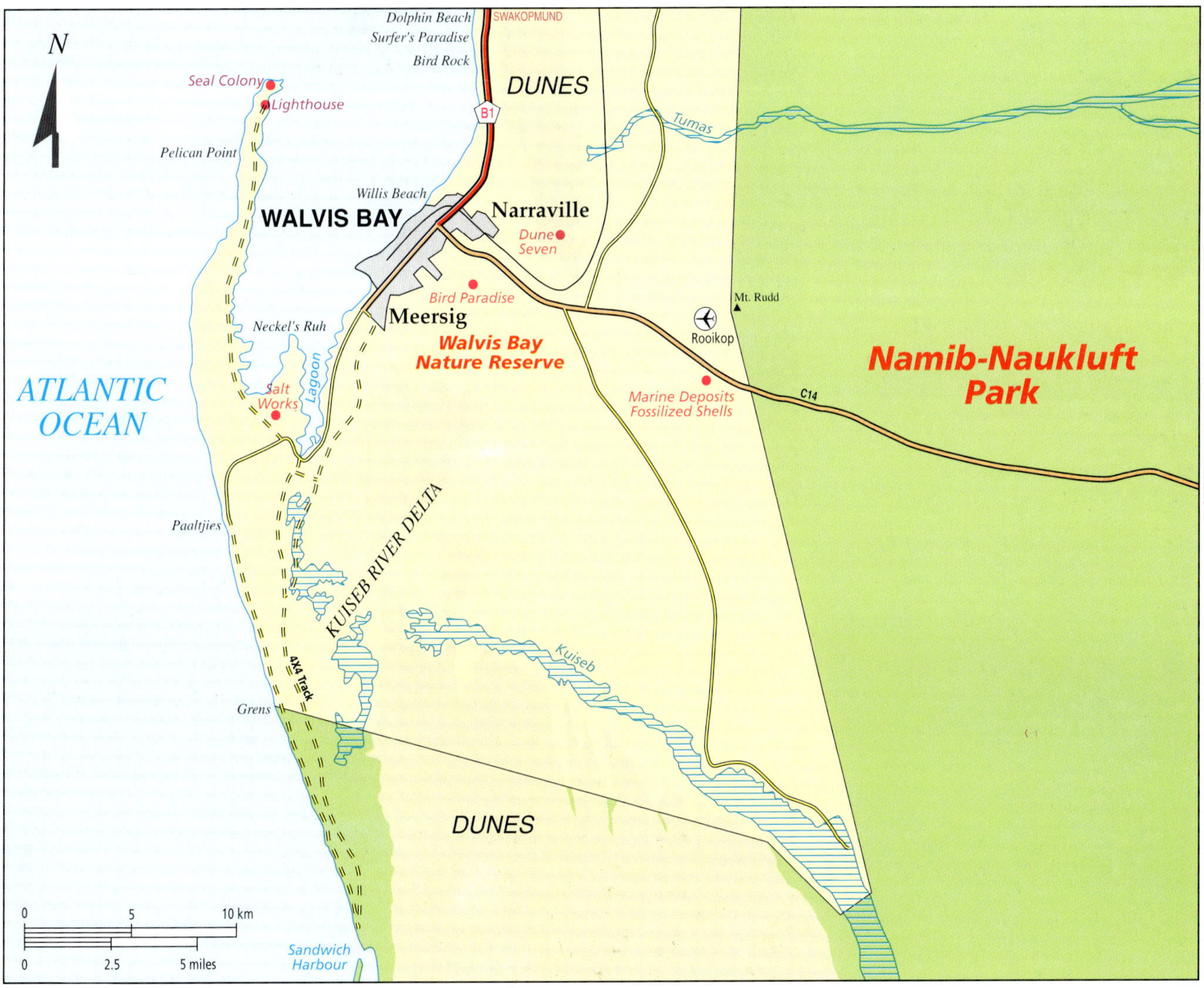

Dolphin Beach
Surfer's Paradise
Bird Rock
SWAKOPMUND
DUNES
B1
Seal Colony
Lighthouse
Pelican Point
Willis Beach
WALVIS BAY
Narraville
Dune Seven
Tumas
Bird Paradise
Meersig
Walvis Bay Nature Reserve
Mt. Rudd
Rooikop
Neckel's Ruh
Salt Works
Lagoon
ATLANTIC OCEAN
Marine Deposits Fossilized Shells
Namib-Naukluft Park
C14
WINDHOEK
Paaltjies
KUISEB RIVER DELTA
Kuiseb
4X4 Track
Grens
DUNES
0
5
10 km
2.5
5 miles
Sandwich Harbour

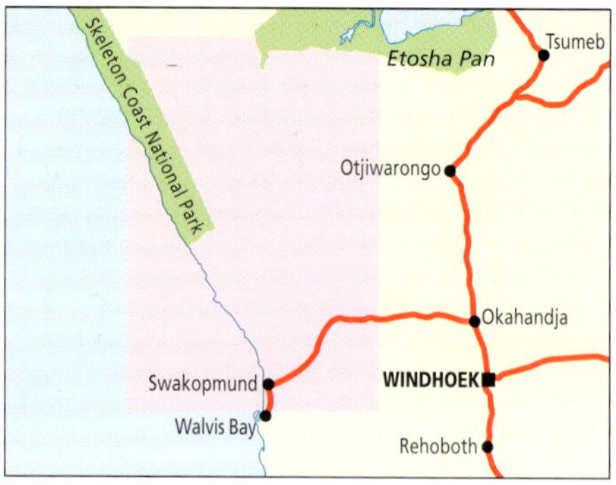

Damaraland

A wealth of rock art (both paintings and engravings), a vast landscape of open plains, table-top mountains and deep gorges, fascinating geological formations, a few challenging hikes and rock-climbing opportunities, and an intriguing variety of game (including desert-dwelling elephants) are the prime attractions of the remote and rugged Damaraland region. Gravel-surface roads, generally in good condition, provide access to all the major sights, and a four-wheel-drive is required only to explore the Palmwag and Etendeka concession areas. A choice of luxury to basic accommodation is offered at several lodges, rest camps and campsites.

Brandberg ('burning mountain'), a mixture of dark basalt and gigantic boulders that become a fiery reddish-orange colour at sunset, is the site of one of the largest collections of rock paintings in the world.

It is a strenuous four-hour walk to view the well-known White Lady frieze. Discovered and identified in 1917 as a depiction of a European woman, it is now generally accepted that the figure is actually that of a man covered in body paint.

About 2400 rock engravings featuring wildlife, animal spoor, abstract patterns and human footprints and handprints have been recorded at Twyfelfontein, farther north. An hour's walk is required to view the engravings.

The domes of Groot Spitzkoppe tower 700m (2296ft) above the surrounding plains in the south of Damaraland. Mountaineers can attempt an ascent of the 1728m (5669ft) peak, while hikers should not miss the climb to Bushman's Paradise, an oasis sheltered by the domes of Pondok Mountain, just east of Spitzkoppe. (Sadly the rock art in the overhang here has been vandalized.)

Close to the dusty town of Khorixas is the Petrified Forest. Among the fossilized remains of the fallen trees are a few specimens of 'living fossils' – welwitschias (*see* page 20).

To the west, near Twyfelfontein, are a peculiar series of dolerite pillars known as the Organ Pipes. Farther on, nature provides a spectacular show in the early morning and late afternoon when the Burnt Mountain (not to be confused with Brandberg farther south) glows as if it is on fire. The rocks here range in colour from black to white with shades of grey, orange and purple. Since Mukurob (*see* page 46) is no longer standing, travellers should not miss a visit to the 35m (115ft) high limestone column, known as Finger Rock, to the east of Khorixas.

Possible sightings of the unique desert-dwelling elephants in the area around Palmwag Lodge and Etendeka Mountain Camp in the remote northern region are a main attraction. Hobatere Lodge (*see* page 11) and Khowarib Schlucht camping site are other accommodation options.

Above: *The typical inselberg of Spitzkoppe was formed by volcanic activity and subsequent erosion.*
Left: *Fan palms look down on the reed huts at Palmwag Lodge, while guests relax in one of the two swimming pools.*
Below left: *Desert-dwelling elephants (see page 30) in the dry Uniab riverbed near Palmwag in northern Damaraland.*

UIS MINE	J	F	M	A	M	J	J	A	S	O	N	D
AVERAGE TEMP. °F	88	88	90	88	84	79	79	81	84	86	90	88
AVERAGE TEMP. °C	31	31	32	31	29	26	26	27	29	30	32	31
Hours of Sun Daily	8	8	8	8	9	9	9	10	9	10	10	11
RAINFALL ins.	1	1.5	1.5	0.5	0	0	0	0	0	0	0	0
RAINFALL mm	24	35	34	10	1	1	0	0	1	1	8	6
Days of Rainfall	12	7	7	2	1	1	0	0	1	1	2	1

Etosha National Park
Old German Fort
Sesfontein
Ongongo Falls
Hot Spring
Khowarib Schlucht
Hoanib
Otjovasandu
C35
Hobatere Lodge
Kunene
Kopermyn
Biermanskool
Weissbrünn
78
Kamanjab
C40
Palmwag Lodge
Damaraland
Endeka Mtn. Camp
Palmwag
Otjikondo
105
MÖWE BAY
Terrace Bay
Uniab
66
45
76
OUTJO
4X4 vehicles
Please do not deviate from existing tracks and do not travel up or down river courses. Strictly no entrance to the Skeleton Coast National Park other than through the official entrance gates.
60
Springbok Gate
Fransfontein
FRANSFONTEIN
1553m
C39
124
Torra Bay
Skeleton Coast National Park
Springbok
232
Petrified Forest
Khorixas
36
Ugab
Finger Rock
Palgrave Pt.
Krone Canyon
Welwitchia Mirabilis
Huab
Twyfelfontein
Burnt Mountain
C35
123
Doros Crater
Goantagab Mine
Ozondati
Brandberg West (Disused Tin Mine)
Ugab
Omatjete
Brandberg
2573m
White Lady Painting
223
Main Gate
Uis Mine
C34
Messum
127
C36
Okombahe
KALKFELD
Orawab
ATLANTIC OCEAN
National West Coast Tourist Recreation Area
C35
ERONGO
SPITZKOPPE
Rock Paintings
1759m
2350m
Etiro
Philips Cave
Cape Cross
Diego Cão's Cross
NAMIB
N
Usakos
Ebony
Aukas
OKAHANDJA/WINDHOEK
Henties Bay
Erongo
Waterbank
Trekkopje
Khan
Arandis
B2
Tsaobis Leopard Nature Park
Wlotzkasbaken
114
Welwitschia Plains
Rock Bay
Rössing
Namib
0
25
50 km
0
25 miles
C34
Swakopmund
Old Railway Station
C28
Swakop
Namib-Naukluft Park
WALVIS BAY

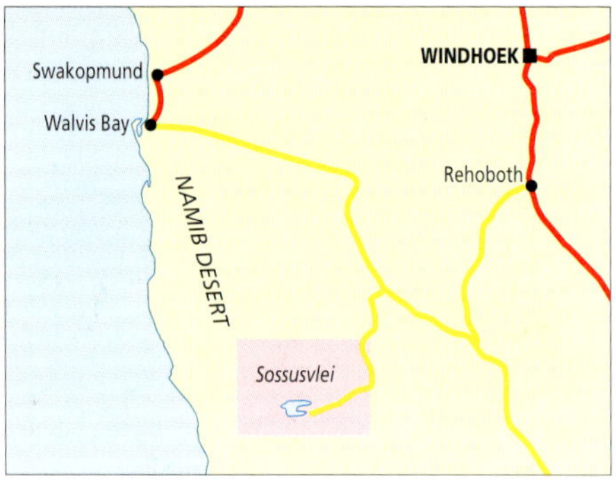

Sesriem and Sossusvlei

The vast dune sea of the Namib Desert is only accessible via Sesriem (see page 39), from where one can visit Sossusvlei, 350km (218 miles) from Swakopmund and 330km (205 miles) from Windhoek. The huge orange sand-dunes at Sossusvlei are one of Namibia's top attractions, and it's not difficult to see why because they are truly spectacular. Alternatively, one can join a novel balloon safari from Kwessiegat, 50km (31 miles) south of Sesriem, and enjoy an exciting aerial view of the dunes and gravel plains of the Namib. A champagne breakfast in the desert and game-viewing on the drive back to the take-off site round off the trip.

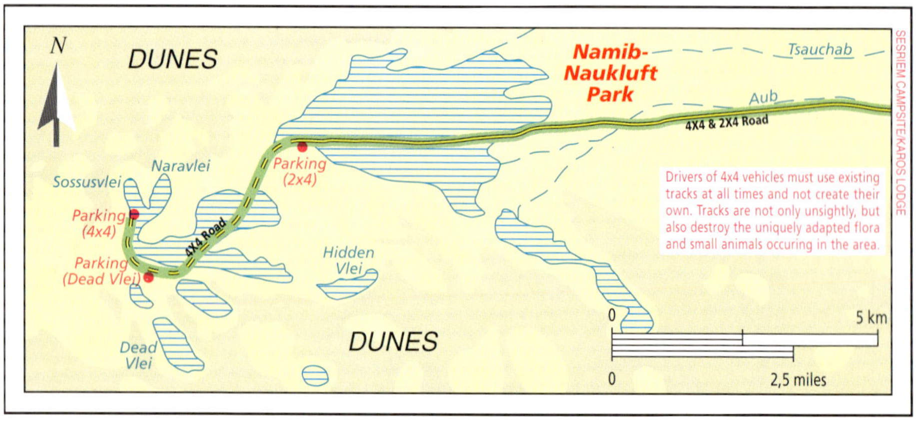

Although it is often claimed that the sand-dunes at Sossusvlei are the highest in the world, they don't really qualify for that distinction as they are not freestanding but rest on a sandstone terrace. Even so, at around 325m (1066ft) high, they are an impressive sight. The brilliant colour of the sand is best seen in the first light of day, and an early start is advisable for the adventurous who want to tackle an ascent of one of the dunes.

It is about a 69km (43 miles) drive along a gravel-surface road to Sossusvlei from Karos Lodge and the campsite at Sesriem, but the last 5km (3 miles) is through heavy sand that only a four-wheel-drive can tackle. En route the Sesriem Canyon (*see* page 39), formed by the Tsauchab River, is about 4km (2.5 miles) south of the pleasantly shaded campsite, and the narrow, deep gorge is especially worth a visit after rain, when it is filled with pools of water.

One would expect a desert to be barren, but the pristine wilderness of the Namib supports a number of endemic animal species. Snakes, such as the side-winding adder, geckos, beetles, spiders, the golden mole, gerbils and larks have all adapted to live in the harsh environment – they live underground or climb onto plants to escape the heat of the sand, and they obtain their precious water supply mostly from fog condensation.

Another fascinating aspect of the Namib is the different shapes of the sand-dunes. Strong southerly winds form crescentic dunes along the coast. Farther east, strong easterly winter winds combine with the southerlies of summer to shape linear transverse dunes; still farther east star dunes with three or more arms radiating from a peak are created by multi-directional winds. The best way to view these vast patterns in the sand is from the air.

SOSSUSVLEI	J	F	M	A	M	J	J	A	S	O	N	D
AVERAGE TEMP. °F	93	91	86	82	75	70	70	75	81	84	91	95
AVERAGE TEMP. °C	34	33	30	28	24	21	21	24	27	29	33	35
Hours of Sun Daily	7	6	7	7	8	8	8	7	6	7	7	7
RAINFALL ins.	0	0	0	0	0	0	0	0	0	0	0	0
RAINFALL mm	1	1	2	2	2	3	2	2	1	1	1	1
Days of Rainfall	1	1	1	1	1	1	0	1	1	0	1	0

The sweeping dunes at Sossusvlei, sculpted by the wind, dwarf a four-wheel-drive crossing the vlei.

Main Map Section Key and Legend

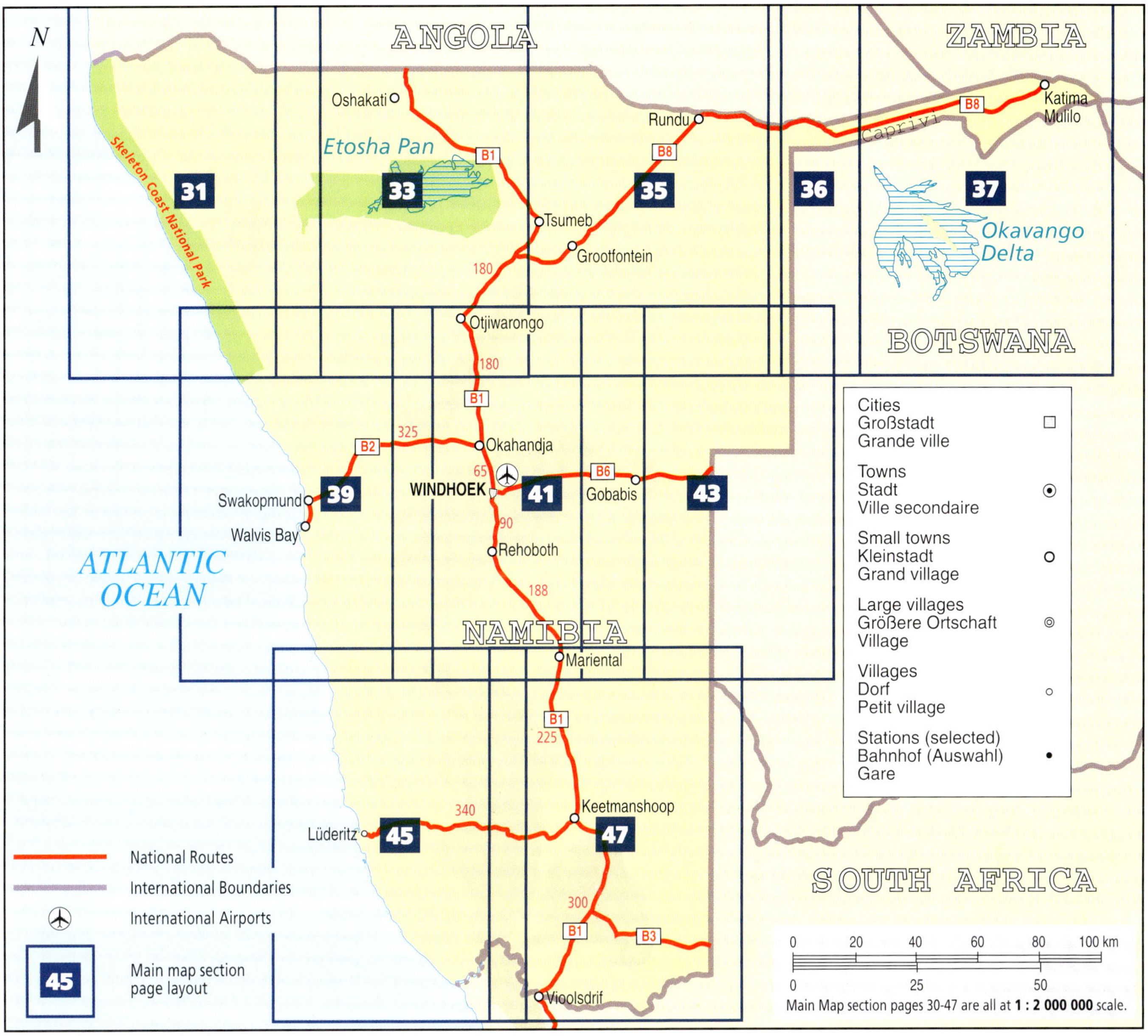

National roads
Nationalrouten
Route nationale

Principal roads
Nationalstraßen
Route de liaison régionale

Main roads
Hauptstraßen
Route principale
Tar Untar

Minor roads
Nebenstraßen
Route secondaire
Tar Untar

Tracks
Sandbahn
Pistes

Route numbers
Routenummern
Numéros de routes
B1 C36

Distances in kilometres
Entfernungen in Kilometern
Distance en kilometres
19 15

Railways
Eisenbahn
Chemin de fer

International boundary
Internationalgrenze
Frontière internationale

Game & nature reserves
Wild und Naturschutzgebiete
Réserves naturelles
Etosha N.P.

Mountain ranges
Gebirge
Chaîne de montagnes
NAUKLUFT

Scenic routes
Malerische Landschaft
Route panoramique

Mountain passes
Bergpässe
Cols
Kuiseb

Border posts
Grenzübergang
Poste de contrôle
Vioolsdrif

Airports
Flughäfen
Aéroports
INT. Other

Places of interest
Sehenswürdigkeiten
Endroit à voir
Sesriem Canyon

Area names
Gebiet
Nom de la région
Damaraland

Peaks in metres
Höhe in Metern
Sommet
Brandberg 2573m

Water features
Gewässer
Hydrographie
River Pan Dam

Major petrol stops
Große Tankstelle
Station-service

Hotels (selected)
Hotel (Auswahl)
Hôtel

Camps
Ferienlager
Camp

Skeleton Coast and Kaokoland

This expansive, remote region is, for the most part, only accessible to four-wheel-drive vehicles and Opuwo is the only settlement where fuel and grocery supplies are available, but it will appeal to those with a spirit of adventure. North of Terrace Bay and south to the Ugab River lies the narrow strip of land called the Skeleton Coast National Park, a solitary coastline known as 'the graveyard of a thousand ships'. Adjacent is scenic and rugged Kaokoland, a vast 49 500km² (19,122 sq miles) area, stretching from the Hoanib River to the Namibian-Angolan border in the north, that is home to the nomadic Himba people and unique desert-dwelling elephants.

Angling is the main attraction in the southern section of the Skeleton Coast National Park, and facilities at Torra Bay and Terrace Bay are geared to fishermen's needs. However, keen walkers can enjoy the two- to three-hour Uniab Delta Walk or the three-day guided Ugab Hiking Trail, a 'no frills attached' hike that should only be tackled by the physically fit.

North of Terrace Bay the fragile wilderness area is protected by restricting access to it, and can only be visited by joining a fly-in safari. A colony of seals at Cape Fria, abstract patterns in the sand, the Clay Castles of the Hoarusib Canyon, roaring dunes in the desert, and the rusting remains of shipwrecks on deserted beaches are the exceptional attractions of this area.

The striking Himba people are nomadic pastoralists who still live much according to age-old tradition in Kaokoland. Carved vegetable ivory ornaments and basket handicrafts can be purchased at the semipermanent Himba settlement of Purros.

The desert-dwelling elephants of Kaokoland are not a separate species, or even subspecies, but have adapted their eating and drinking habits so that they can survive in a desert environment. Of the 250-325 of these gigantic, slow-moving mammals, only about 50 live in the true desert environment between the Hoanib and Hoarusib rivers.

Visitors to Sesfontein can see the ruins of a German fort dating back to 1905-6. Also in the area is the settlement of Warmquelle, the site of a tree-shaded lukewarm thermal spring, and the delightful Ongongo Falls where one can cool off in the crystal-clear pool.

The Kunene River forms the boundary between Namibia and Angola, and was a war zone until the end of the 1980s. However, tourist development is planned in this beautiful area, and already, rafting trips on the river are on offer. The spectacular Epupa Falls and well-known Ruacana Falls, dry for most of the year but impressive after good rains, are the main attractions of the region.

MÖWE BAY	J	F	M	A	M	J	J	A	S	O	N	D
AVERAGE TEMP. °F	68	68	68	66	64	64	61	59	59	61	63	66
AVERAGE TEMP. °C	20	20	20	19	18	18	16	15	15	16	17	19
Hours of Sun Daily	7	8	8	6	5	4	4	4	4	6	8	8
RAINFALL ins.	0	0	0.5	0	0	0	0	0	0	0	0	0
RAINFALL mm	4	5	10	1	1	1	0	0	0	1	0	0
Days of Rainfall	1	2	2	1	1	1	0	0	0	1	0	0

Top: *Seabirds perch on a rusting, abandoned ship on Namibia's notorious Skeleton Coast.*
Above left: *The cascading waters of Epupa Falls.*
Above: *Remote Kaokoland – an immense, arid tract of land where roads are often mere tracks.*
Left: *A graceful Himba women in traditional dress and adornments.*

Main Map Section

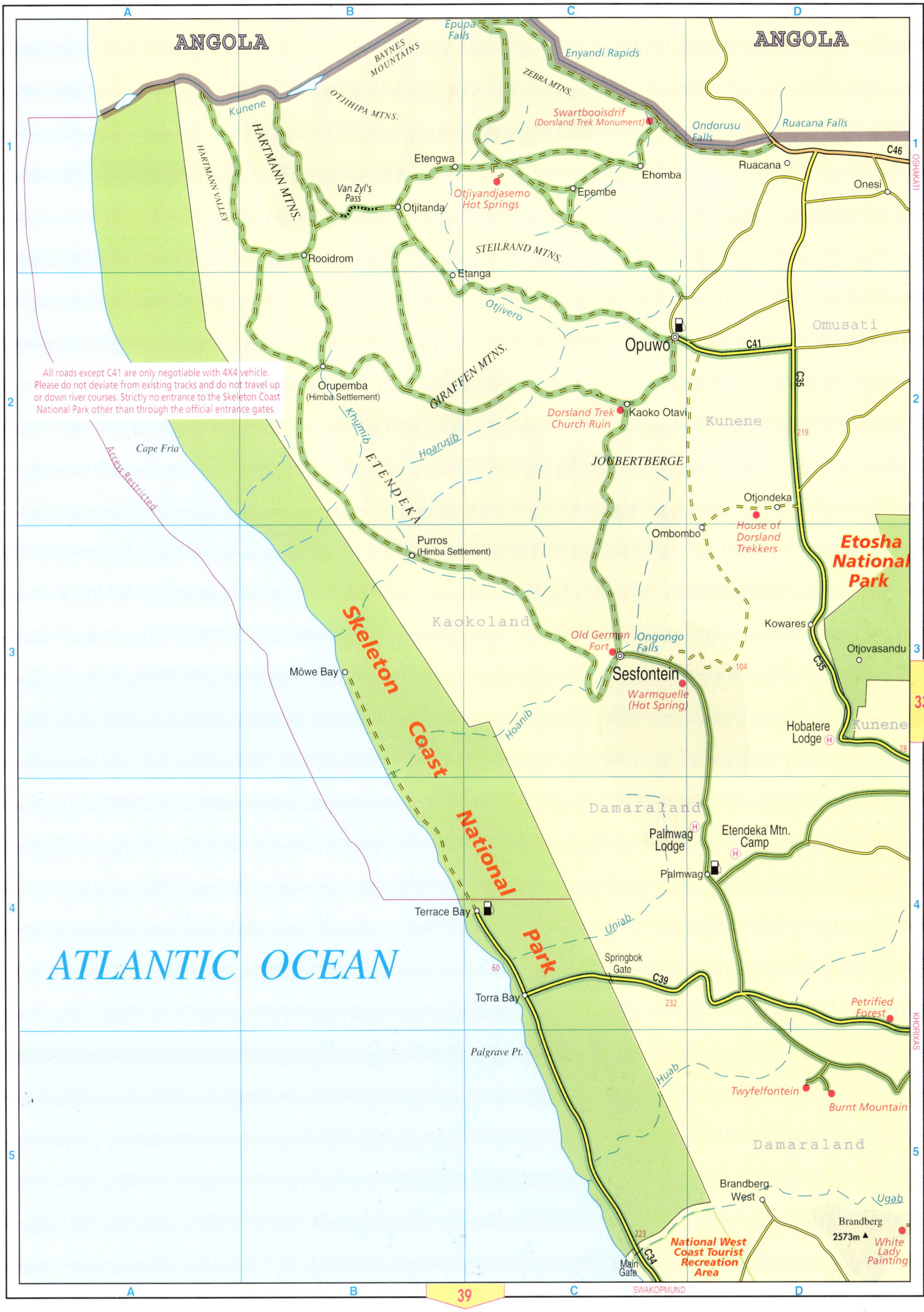

33

39

Etosha and the North

Etosha National Park (see pages 10-11) is a mere five hours' drive from Windhoek, but attractions en route, including rock art in the Erongo region, the pleasant, historic town of Omaruru (see page 41), and rare animals in the Waterberg Plateau Park, entice the traveller to make it a leisurely drive. From Etosha the B1 leads to the North, the most densely populated region in Namibia, yet still relatively unexplored by tourists. The C38 offers an alternative route from Otjiwarongo to Etosha, and access to the wonders of Damaraland (see page 26), while places of interest around Grootfontein (see page 34), about 87km (54 miles) east of Otavi, are worth a visit.

Buildings of historical interest in Omaruru include the Rhenish Mission House (1871), now a museum, the Rhenish Mission Church (1872), and the Franke Tower (1908), which commemorates the relief of the siege of Omaruru during the Herero Uprising of 1904. October is the best month to visit as the local Herero, known as the 'White Flag Herero', conduct a colourful procession through the town to pay tribute to their leader, Wilhelm Zeraua.

West of Omaruru is the Erongo Mountain, site of the 'White Elephant' rock painting in Phillip's Cave, and near Kalkfeld, about 68km (42 miles) north of Omaruru, one can see footprints that a three-toed dinosaur left in the red Etjo sandstone over 150 million years ago. The luxurious Mount Etjo Safari Lodge, situated nearby, offers guided walks, and game-viewing drives in open safari vehicles, and at Okonjima guest farm, from a hide in the mountains, visitors can watch leopard feeding.

Guided wilderness trails and rare game species, including black and white rhino, roan and sable antelope, are drawcards at Waterberg Plateau Park, which is dominated by a steep-sided plateau. Red hartebeest, eland and kudu also inhabit the park, and endangered Cape vultures can be observed from a hide.

Lake Otjikoto and nearby Lake Guinas lie alongside the main road from Tsumeb to Etosha and are home to the endangered *Otjikoto tilapia*. The lakes are actually deep sinkholes and weapons dumped in Otjikoto in 1915 by retreating German soldiers are on display in the Tsumeb Museum (*see* page 34).

Dusty towns abuzz with people, domestic animals, taxis driven at daredevil speed, and brightly painted informal trading stores known as *cuca* shops are characteristic of the North. Owambo handicrafts and a host of waterbirds at Lake Oponono are highlights of a tour of the region.

A four-wheel-drive and a good sense of direction are essential to explore the scenic beauty of the North – numerous tracks traverse the land, and the pans and *oshanas* (a network of shallow watercourses) south of Oshakati are flooded after summer rains.

Above: *Guests at the luxurious Mount Etjo Safari Lodge can spot game, such as white rhino, lion, elephant and Damara dik-dik, on a game-viewing drive, on foot or from one of the hides.*
Above left: *The 25m (82ft) stretch of fossil tracks of a two-legged, three-toed dinosaur embedded in the red Etjo sandstone on Otjihaenamaparero farm near Kalkfeld.*
Left: *Hikers on a guided wilderness trail through the Waterberg Plateau Park stop to admire the scenery.*

ETOSHA PAN	J	F	M	A	M	J	J	A	S	O	N	D
AVERAGE TEMP. °F	79	77	75	73	66	61	61	66	73	79	79	79
AVERAGE TEMP. °C	26	25	24	23	19	16	16	19	23	26	26	26
Hours of Sun Daily	8	7	8	9	10	10	10	10	9	9	9	10
RAINFALL ins.	3	4	3	1	1	0	0	0	0	0	1	2.5
RAINFALL mm	75	109	75	26	18	1	0	0	2	7	31	68
Days of Rainfall	15	13	11	6	1	0	0	0	1	5	9	13

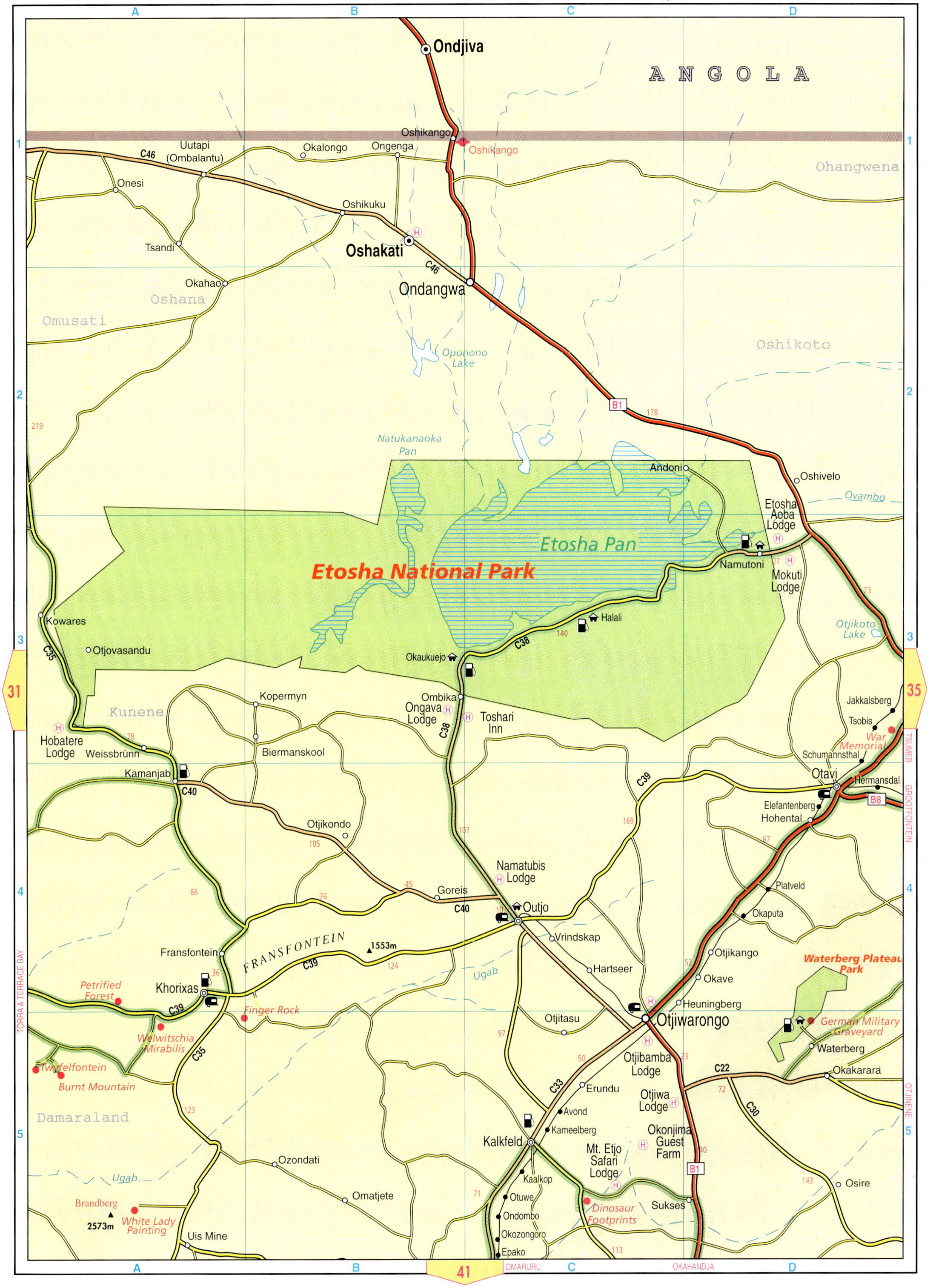
ANGOLA
Ondjiva
Oshikango
Okalongo
Ongenga
Uutapi (Ombalantu)
C46
Onesi
Oshikuku
Tsandi
Oshakati
Ondangwa
Okahao
Oshana
Omusati
Ohangwena
Oshikoto
Opono Lake
Natukanaoka Pan
B1
Andoni
Oshivelo
Ovambo
Etosha Aoba Lodge
Etosha Pan
Etosha National Park
Namutoni
Mokuti Lodge
Halali
C38
Okaukuejo
Kowares
C35
Otjovasandu
Otjikoto Lake
Ombika
Ongava Lodge
Toshari Inn
Kopermyn
Kunene
Hobatere Lodge
Weissbrünn
Biermanskool
Kamanjab
C40
Jakkalsberg
Tsobis
War Memorial
Schumannsthal
Otavi
Hermansdal
B8
Elefantenberg
Hohental
C39
Otjikondo
Namatubis Lodge
Goreis
Outjo
Vrindskap
Platveld
Okaputa
Otjikango
Fransfontein
FRANSFONTEIN
1553m
Ugab
Hartseer
Okave
Waterberg Plateau Park
Petrified Forest
Khorixas
Finger Rock
Heuningberg
Otjiwarongo
German Military Graveyard
Welwitschia Mirabilis
Otjitasu
Otjibamba Lodge
Waterberg
Twyfelfontein
Burnt Mountain
C22
Okakarara
C33
Erundu
Otjiwa Lodge
C30
Damaraland
Avond
Kameelberg
Okonjima Guest Farm
Kalkfeld
Mt. Etjo Safari Lodge
Ozondati
Kaalkop
Osire
Brandberg
2573m
White Lady Painting
Omatjete
Otuwe
Dinosaur Footprints
Sukses
Ondombo
Okozongoro
Uis Mine
Epako
31
35
41
TORRA & TERRACE BAY
TSUMEB
GROOTFONTEIN
OTJINENE
OMARURU
OKAHANDJA

Bushmanland and Okavango

Tsumeb and Grootfontein are, respectively, the gateways to Etosha (see pages 10-11) and north-eastern Namibia (see page 36). Of the 213 minerals contained in the ore body mined at Tsumeb, 40 are only found here. The buildings that date back to the early 1900s and a museum featuring a display of minerals and gemstones demonstrate that this is a mining town. A historic fort in tree-lined Grootfontein serves as a museum that depicts the early history of the district and includes a display on wagon-making. If you are in the area, pay a visit to the Hoba Meteorite. Estimated to be over 190 million years old, it is the largest in the world and weighs about 60 tonnes.

Most of the roads in Bushmanland are mere tracks that are not signposted, and Tsumkwe is the only place where fuel and basic supplies are available, so a four-wheel-drive and wilderness 'know-how' are essential.

Large baobab trees are a feature of the landscape and of special interest is the Holboom (Hollow Tree) near Tjokwe, and the Grootboom (Large Tree), between Tjokwe and Kaudom, with an immense circumference of over 30m (98ft).

Bushmanland also has its open plains, woodlands and seasonally inundated pans. Although game is not plentiful here, the pans attract giraffe, elephant, roan antelope, wild dog, lion, leopard and hyena in search of water in the dry season, and, when flooded in the wet season (December to May), they are visited by thousands of waterbirds.

The Ju!Wasi San people or Bushmen inhabit eastern Bushmanland, but they are becoming westernized and no longer wear traditional dress or live exclusively by hunting and gathering. Even so, one should show respect and courtesy to these people and take care to leave as little evidence as possible of your visit.

North of Bushmanland is the Kaudom Game Park, one of Namibia's finest, though little visited, wildlife areas. Once again, a four-wheel-drive is required to negotiate the sandy network of roads, and facilities at the two rest camps are very basic. Wild dog, lion, sable, tsessebe, kudu, wildebeest and elephant are some of the game that can be seen in the park.

Rundu, on the banks of the Kavango River after which the region is named, is the administrative centre of the area, and of special interest here is the Mbangura Woodcarvers' Co-operative where attractive Kavango wood handicrafts ranging from animal sculptures to furniture can be purchased. Human faces are a popular subject for the woodcarvers, who work mainly in teak.

Top: *The appealing, sun-wrinkled face of this Ju!Wasi woman is adorned with make-up and bead-work, a tradition that is no longer the norm among San people, who are adopting a Western way of life.*
Above left: *Elephant are usually easily spotted in Kaudom Game Park, especially in the dry winter months when they stay close to waterholes.*

Above right: *A four-wheel-drive vehicle slowly negotiates a sandy track in Kaudom. Winter is the prime time to visit the park as the summer rains not only result in muddy tracks, but it is more difficult to spot game in the summer months (even giraffe) as tall grass conceals the animals and the availability of ground water disperses them.*

TSUMEB	J	F	M	A	M	J	J	A	S	O	N	D
AVERAGE TEMP. °F	77	75	73	72	50	61	61	66	73	79	77	77
AVERAGE TEMP. °C	25	24	23	22	10	16	16	19	23	26	25	25
Hours of Sun Daily	8	7	8	8	9	9	9	8	7	8	8	8
RAINFALL ins.	4.5	5	3	1.5	0	0	0	0	0	0.5	2	3
RAINFALL mm	119	124	83	39	7	1	0	0	2	17	59	84
Days of Rainfall	15	13	11	6	1	0	0	0	1	5	9	13

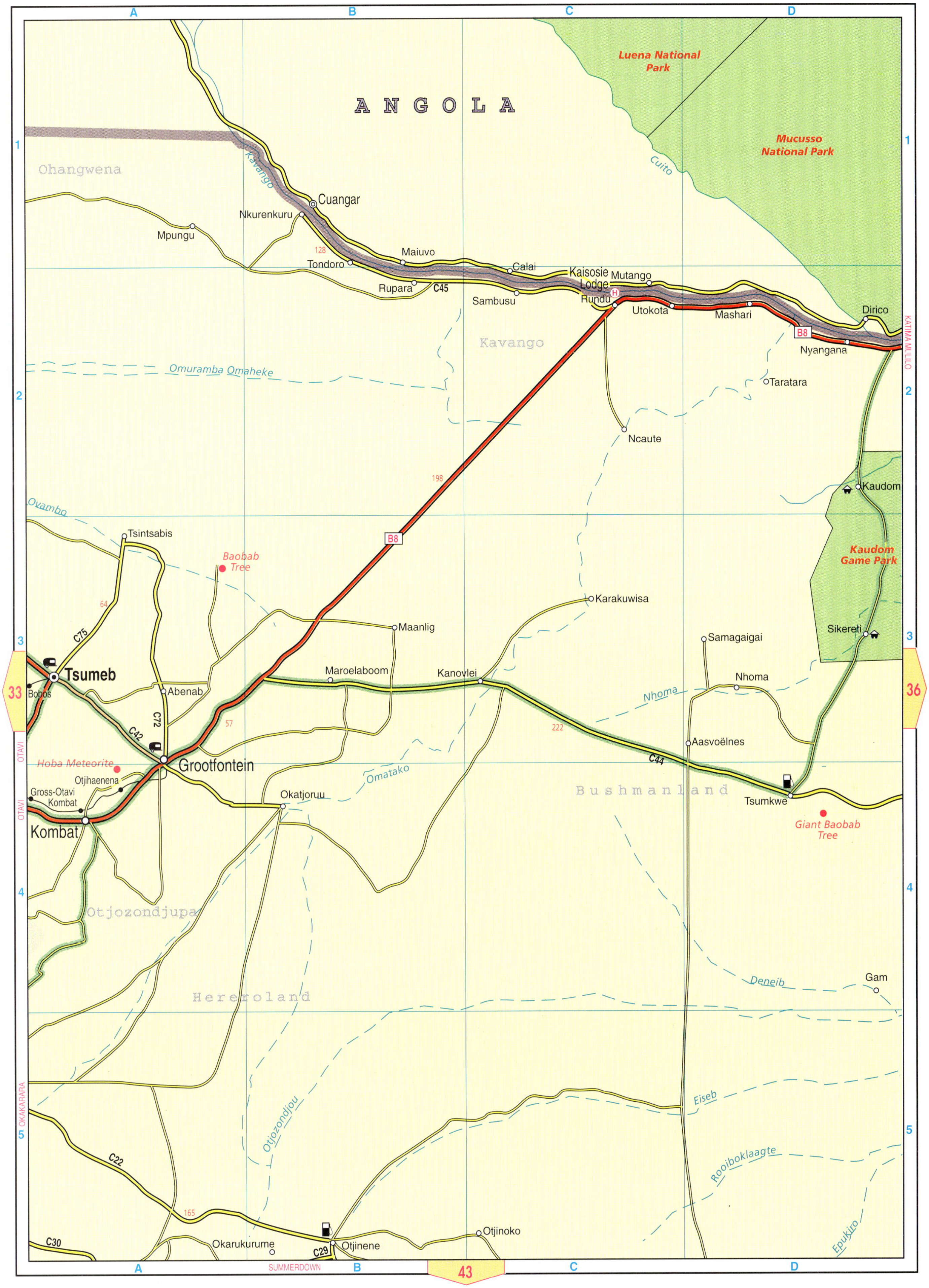
ANGOLA
Luena National Park
Mucusso National Park
Ohangwena
Kavango
Cuito
Cuangar
Nkurenkuru
Mpungu
Tondoro
Maiuvo
Calai
Kaisosie Lodge
Mutango
Rundu
Rupara
C45
Sambusu
Utokota
Mashari
Dirico
B8
Nyangana
Kavango
Omuramba Omaheke
Taratara
Ncaute
198
Kaudom
Ovambo
Tsintsabis
Baobab Tree
Kaudom Game Park
Karakuwisa
Maanlig
Sikereti
Samagaigai
C75
64
Tsumeb
Bobos
Abenab
Maroelaboom
Kanovlei
Nhoma
Nhoma
C72
57
C42
222
Aasvoëlnes
Hoba Meteorite
Grootfontein
Omatako
C44
Otjihaenena
Gross-Otavi
Kombat
Okatjoruu
Bushmanland
Tsumkwe
Kombat
Giant Baobab Tree
Otjozondjupa
Hereroland
Deneib
Gam
Eiseb
Otjozondjou
Rooiboklaagte
C22
165
Epukiro
C30
Okarukurume
C29
Otjinene
Otjinoko
A
B
C
D
1
2
3
4
5
OTAVI
OKAKARARA
KATIMA MULILO
SUMMERDOWN
33
36
43

Caprivi

Caprivi is a narrow stretch of land bounded in the west and east by the Kavango and Kwando rivers. Katima Mulilo is the region's administrative and tourist centre, and serves as a gateway to the magnificent Victoria Falls in Zimbabwe and the world-renowned Chobe National Park in Botswana. The liberation struggle, fought mainly in the north, restricted tourism here until the late 1980s, but visitors are now discovering the many attractions of the Caprivi region – a prolific birdlife (including the rare black-cheeked lovebird), three game sanctuaries, tiger fishing and a network of waterways that can be navigated with a variety of river-boats.

About 200km (124 miles) east of Rundu is Popa Falls, a 1km (0.6 miles) wide course of cascading water. A tree-shaded rest camp is situated on the banks of the Kavango River and alternative accommodation is provided at Suclabo Lodge, about 1km (0.6 miles) downstream. Both can be used as a base for a tour of the relatively small Mahango Game Park.

Woodlands, floodplains and grassy, seasonal river courses in the park are the habitat for large herds of elephant, red lechwe, reedbuck and waterbuck, Chobe bushbuck, and the occasional lion. In the summer, migrants bring the number of resident bird species close to 400.

An astonishing 70% of Namibia's bird species are found in the Caprivi, many of which only occur in this part of the country. Look out for the African skimmer, slaty egret, long-toed plover, coppery-tailed coucal, western banded snake eagle, coppery sunbird, greater swamp warbler and Bradfield's hornbill.

The densely wooded Caprivi Game Park is mostly inaccessible to tourists, but the Mudumu and Mamili national parks are highlights of a visit to Caprivi. At Mudumu, look out for Burchell's zebra, red lechwe, sitatunga and roan antelope, as well as the African fish eagle, Narina trogon and Pel's fishing owl. Mamili is a world of reed-lined waterways and wooded islands called the Linyanti Swamps.

Namushasha Lodge, 20km (12 miles) south of Kongola, and Lianshulu Lodge, in Mudumu National Park, as well as campsites at both parks, provide accommodation and offer a variety of activities. Of special interest at Lianshulu is the Lizauli Traditional Village, where the local way of life is demonstrated.

The Caprivi Art Centre at Katima Mulilio sells ethnic handicrafts, and the Zambezi Lodge, which has a floating bar, and a golf course that is sometimes visited by hippos, and rustic Hippo Lodge offer accommodation on the banks of the Zambezi River.

Exploring the waterways on a variety of craft, from the traditional *mokoro* (dugout canoe) to the luxurious *Zambezi Queen*, is a must. Kalizo Safari Camp, 37km (23 miles) downstream, organizes angling and canoeing safaris.

This double-decker observation platform floating on the tranquil Kwando River provides guests at Lianshulu Lodge in Mudumu National Park with the opportunity to enjoy game-viewing on the reed-lined waterway in leisurely comfort, and is also the vehicle for memorable African-style sunset cruises.

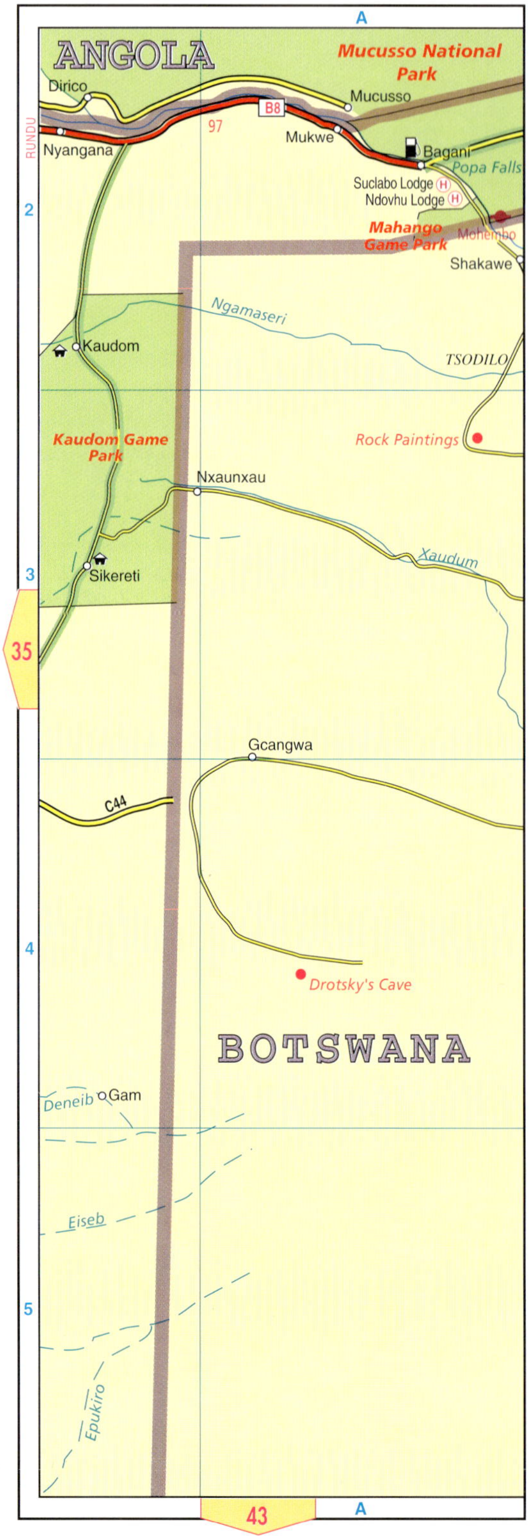

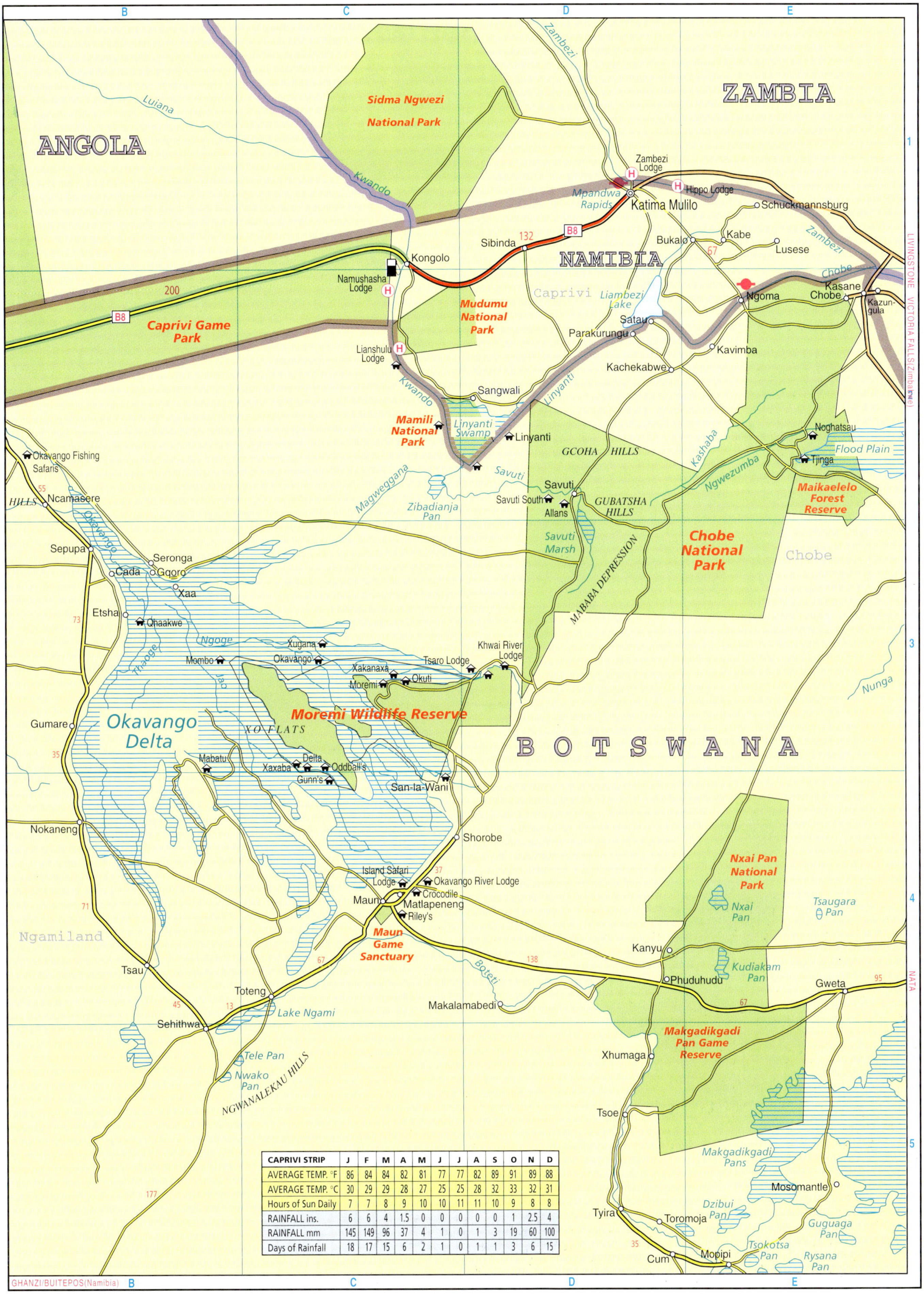

CAPRIVI STRIP	J	F	M	A	M	J	J	A	S	O	N	D
AVERAGE TEMP. °F	86	84	84	82	81	77	77	82	89	91	89	88
AVERAGE TEMP. °C	30	29	29	28	27	25	25	28	32	33	32	31
Hours of Sun Daily	7	7	8	9	10	10	11	11	10	9	8	8
RAINFALL ins.	6	6	4	1.5	0	0	0	0	0	1	2.5	4
RAINFALL mm	145	149	96	37	4	1	0	1	3	19	60	100
Days of Rainfall	18	17	15	6	2	1	0	1	1	3	6	15

National West Coast Tourist Recreation Area

North of Swakopmund and the Namib-Naukluft Park (see pages 20 and 22), bounded in the west by the Atlantic Ocean and in the east by Damaraland (see page 26) and the Erongo region (see page 32), is a surf fisherman's paradise – the National West Coast Tourist Recreation Area. The fragile ecology of this 200km (124 miles) strip of coast is contantly under threat because of its popularity and accessibility. A sinister-looking 'skeleton' gate at the Ugab River in the north marks the entrance to the Skeleton Coast National Park (see page 30).

Several campsites, the largest and best equipped being Mile Four, offer basic lodgings for anglers along the coast. Wlotkazbaken and Henties Bay are the only settlements, and only the latter has facilities for tourists, including a golf course with grass greens but sand fairways.

Galjoen, kob (also called kabeljou), white steenbras and blacktail are popular catches, although angling regulations are strictly enforced to prevent the over-exploitation of this precious natural resource.

Cape Cross Seal Reserve, 120km (74.5 miles) north of Swakopmund, is one of 16 breeding colonies of the Cape fur seal along the Namibian coast. Up to an estimated 100,000 seals can be found here at any one time, and, after obtaining a permit, one can observe them at leisure from a viewpoint behind a wall every day of the week except Friday. Two stone crosses, or *padrões*, at Cape Cross are a reminder of the seafaring explorers of yesteryear. One is an authentic replica of the *padrão* erected in 1486 by Diego Cão, probably the first European to set foot on Namibian soil. The other is a granite replica that replaced the original when it was removed to Germany in 1893.

Up to 80% of the world's estimated 7000 Damara terns visit the coast to breed each year during September and October. They build their nests up to 5km (3 miles) inland on the gravel plains and between the dunes of the desert, and lay a single egg. Also of interest in the area are the most extensive lichen fields in the world. The estimated 100 species of this strange plant form – a symbiotic mixture of fungi and algae – survive on the fog that covers the coast for around 100 days a year. Early morning is the best time to see the range of hues that the varieties display, as they lose their colour when they dry out in the heat of the sun.

Above right: *Each year a large colony of seals congregates on the beach at Cape Cross to breed.*
Above: *Seal pups are born from late November, and stay close together for protection against predators while their mothers go out to sea to feed.*
Right: *The two padrões at Cape Cross. The authentic dolerite replica in the foreground was based on a plaster cast of the original.*

SWAKOPMUND	J	F	M	A	M	J	J	A	S	O	N	D
AVERAGE TEMP. °F	63	64	63	60	60	59	55	55	55	57	60	63
AVERAGE TEMP. °C	17	18	17	16	16	15	13	13	13	14	15	17
Hours of Sun Daily	7	6	7	7	8	8	8	7	6	7	7	7
SEA TEMP. °F	68	66	64	63	63	59	59	59	59	59	61	61
SEA TEMP. °C	20	19	18	17	17	15	15	15	15	15	16	16
RAINFALL ins.	0	0	0	0	0	0	0	0	0	0	0	0
RAINFALL mm	1	1	7	1	0	3	0	0	0	0	0	0
Days of Rainfall	1	1	1	1	0	1	0	0	1	0	1	0

31
45
41
A
B
C
D
1
2
3
4
5
Palgrave Pt.
Skeleton Coast Nat. Park
Huab
Twyfelfontein
Burnt Mountain
Damaraland
Brandberg West
Ugab
Brandberg
2573m
White Lady Painting
Uis Mine
Ozondati
Omatjete
Otjitasu
Avond
Kameelberg
Kalkfeld
Kaalkop
Otuwe
Ondombo
Okozongoro
Epako
Okakombo
Okombahe
Omaruru
Von Franke Tower
Norman
Erongo
Etiro
Erongo
2350m
Ameib Ranch
Philips Cave
Albrechts
Vogelsang
Wilhelmstal
Karibib
Usakos
Aukas
Ebony
Spitzkoppe
1759m
Rock Paintings
Main Gate
National West Coast Tourist Recreation Area
NAMIB
Cape Cross
Diego Cão's Cross
Henties Bay
Erongo
Waterbank
Trekkopje
Khan
Arandis
Tsaobis Leopard Nature Park
Powder Tower
Otjimbingwe
Welwitschia Plains
Wlotzkasbaken
Rock Bay
Rössing
Namib
Wüstenquell Guest Farm
ATLANTIC OCEAN
Swakopmund
Old Railway Station
Swakop
Bosua Pass
KHOMAS HOCHLAND
Walvis Bay
Old Rhenish Mission Church
Namib-Naukluft Park
Kuiseb Pass
Gamsberg Pass
Kuiseb Canyon
Sandwich Bay
TROPIC OF CAPRICORN
Gaub Pass
Kuiseb
Spreetshoogte Pass
Nauchas
Swartfontein Guest Farm
Conception Bay
Tsondab Vlei
Tsondab
Solitaire
Remhoogte
Ababis Guest Farm
Namib Naukluft Lodge
1973m
NAUKLUFT
Meob Bay
Karos
Sesriem
Sesriem Canyon
Tsauchab
Sossusvlei
Sandunes
Hot Air Balloon Safaris
TSARISBERGE
ZARIS
OTJIWARONGO
OKAHANDJA
REHOBOTH
MALTAHÖHE
C34
C35
C36
C33
C32
C28
C14
C26
C24
B2
223
123
127
71
54
66
50
114
34
168
164
84
63
97

Central Highlands

Windhoek (see page 8) is conveniently placed as a base for exploring the central highlands – sports enthusiasts can enjoy watersports at Hardap Dam while the thermal springs at Rehoboth and Gross Barmen are a treat. Game-viewing and bird-watching can be conducted on foot at Hardap Game Reserve or from a vehicle at the Intu Afrika Game Lodge, and the colourful Herero processions at Okahandja are a photographer's delight. For those who want to venture farther afield, a drive through the Khomas Hochland along one of the mountain passes (see page 6) leads to the wonders of the Namib-Naukluft Park (see pages 20 and 28).

A stop at Rehoboth, 80km (50 miles) south of Windhoek, is recommended for a picnic next to the Oanob Dam, a therapeutic swim at the Reho Spa hot-water springs, or a meander through the interesting Rehoboth Museum where the history of the Baster people, who settled here in 1870, is depicted.

Farther south, near Mariental, the Intu Afrika Game Lodge offers game-viewing drives in the Kalahari and luxury accommodation, and Hardap Dam Recreation Resort is a popular venue for watersports, fishing, and game-viewing and bird-watching walks (but walkers should look out for and avoid the few black rhino) in the game reserve. The view over the dam from the restaurant at Hardap is superb.

Not-to-be-missed occasions are the colourful processions in Okahandja, 70km (43 miles) north of Windhoek. In August the Red Flag Herero pay tribute to their forefathers – the men don military gear for the event, while the women look splendid in their Victorian-style dress. The Green Flag Herero, or Mbanderu, pay tribute to their forefathers in a procession in June. Visitors shopping for curios should visit the Kavango woodcarvers' market.

Gross Barmen, 24km (15 miles) west of Okahandja, is the site of another thermal spring. The resort also offers a variety of accommodation options, a restaurant, shop, sports facilities and a filling station.

Farther west is the Tsaobis Leopard Nature Park. Situated in rugged mountainous countryside, the park was established as a sanctuary for leopard but also includes other wildlife such as springbok, kudu, red hartebeest and gemsbok. The park is open throughout the year, it has ten fully-equipped bungalows, a swimming pool and offers unaccompanied walks and game-viewing drives.

From Windhoek, scenic mountain passes through the Khomas Hochland lead to some of the major attractions in the Namib-Naukluft Park. The spectacular Kuiseb Canyon, 230km (143 miles) from the capital, is best viewed from Carp Cliff in the late afternoon. Although the Kuiseb River and its many tributaries are usually dry, after good rains a torrent of water rushes through the canyon and washes away the sand from the encroaching dunes that threaten to engulf the gravel plains to the north. Farther south, the Naukluft Mountain complex is a sanctuary for Hartmann's mountain zebra and other game, and the starting point for two challenging one-day hiking trails.

Above left: *The temperature of the thermal outdoor pool at Gross Barmen is about 29°C (52°F).*
Above: *The undulating hills and valleys of the Khomas Hochland are covered in a luxuriant carpet of green after the summer rains.*

WINDHOEK	J	F	M	A	M	J	J	A	S	O	N	D
AVERAGE TEMP. °F	74	73	70	66	61	55	55	61	66	72	72	75
AVERAGE TEMP. °C	24	23	21	19	16	13	13	16	19	22	22	24
Hours of Sun Daily	9	9	8	9	10	10	10	11	10	10	10	10
RAINFALL ins.	3	3	3	1.5	0	0	0	0	0	0.5	1	2
RAINFALL mm	78	77	79	38	7	1	1	1	3	11	27	42
Days of Rainfall	11	11	11	5	2	1	1	0	1	3	5	7

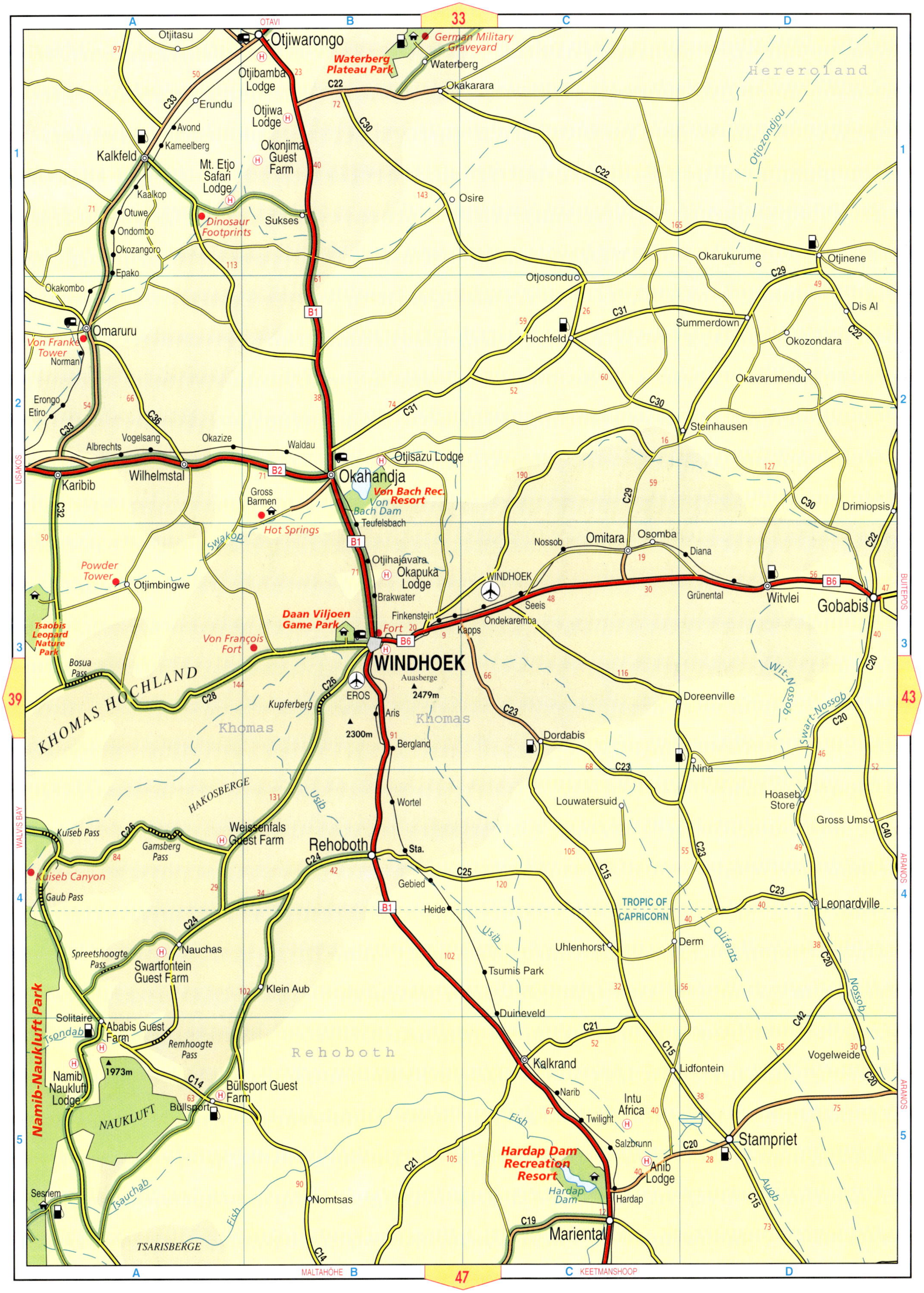
33
OTAVI
Otjitasu
Otjiwarongo
Otjibamba Lodge
Erundu
Avond
Kameelberg
Kalkfeld
Otjiwa Lodge
Okonjima Guest Farm
Mt. Etjo Safari Lodge
Kaalkop
Otuwe
Ondombo
Okozangoro
Epako
Okakombo
Omaruru
Von Franke Tower
Norman
Erongo
Etiro
Dinosaur Footprints
Sukses
Waterberg Plateau Park
German Military Graveyard
Waterberg
Okakarara
Hereroland
Otjozondjou
Osire
Okarukurume
Otjinene
Otjosondu
Hochfeld
Summerdown
Dis Al
Okozondara
Okavarumendu
Steinhausen
Drimiopsis
Albrechts
Vogelsang
Okazize
Waldau
Karibib
Wilhelmstal
Okahandja
Otjisazu Lodge
Von Bach Rec. Resort
Von Bach Dam
Gross Barmen
Hot Springs
Teufelsbach
Swakop
Powder Tower
Otjimbingwe
Otjihajavara
Okapuka Lodge
Brakwater
Nossob
Omitara
Osomba
Diana
WINDHOEK
Grünental
Witvlei
Gobabis
Tsaobis Leopard Nature Park
Daan Viljoen Game Park
Von François Fort
Fort
Finkenstein
Seeis
Ondekaremba
Kapps
Bosua Pass
KHOMAS HOCHLAND
EROS
Auasberge
2479m
Aris
2300m
Kupferberg
Khomas
Bergland
Dordabis
Doreenville
Wit-Nossob
Swart-Nossob
Nina
Hoaseb Store
Gross Ums
Louwatersuid
HAKOSBERGE
Usib
Wortel
Weissenfals Guest Farm
Kuiseb Pass
Gamsberg Pass
Rehoboth
Sta.
Kuiseb Canyon
Gaub Pass
Gebied
Heide
TROPIC OF CAPRICORN
Leonardville
Derm
Uhlenhorst
Olifants
Spreetshoogte Pass
Nauchas
Swartfontein Guest Farm
Tsumis Park
Klein Aub
Duineveld
Nossob
Solitaire
Tsondab
Ababis Guest Farm
Remhoogte Pass
Rehoboth
Kalkrand
Lidfontein
Vogelweide
Namib-Naukluft Park
Namib Naukluft Lodge
1973m
NAUKLUFT
Büllsport Guest Farm
Bullsport
Narib
Twilight
Intu Africa
Fish
Salzbrunn
Stampriet
Hardap Dam Recreation Resort
Hardap Dam
Anib Lodge
Hardap
Auob
Sesriem
Tsauchab
Fish
Nomtsas
Mariental
TSARISBERGE
MALTAHÖHE
47
KEETMANSHOOP
USAKOS
WALVIS BAY
BUITEPOS
ARANOS
39
43
A
B
C
D
1
2
3
4
5
B1
B2
B6
C14
C15
C19
C20
C21
C22
C23
C24
C25
C26
C28
C29
C30
C31
C32
C33
C36
C40
C42

Kalahari

The vast wilderness area of the Kalahari covers eastern Namibia and most of Botswana, extending into neighbouring South Africa to the south, and Angola plus a corner of Zimbabwe to the north. More commonly referred to as arid savanna woodlands, the region is characterized by hardy acacias, and specifically camelthorn trees. To the south, the typical east-west oriented red Kalahari sand-dunes are intersected by dune 'streets' – forested corridors or valleys along dry riverbeds. Gobabis is a pleasant place to stop for travellers en route to Botswana via the Trans-Kalahari Highway, which is still in the process of being tarred.

GOBABIS	J	F	M	A	M	J	J	A	S	O	N	D
AVERAGE TEMP. °F	86	84	82	79	75	70	70	75	82	86	86	88
AVERAGE TEMP. °C	30	29	28	26	24	21	21	24	28	30	30	31
Hours of Sun Daily	9	9	8	9	10	10	10	11	10	10	10	10
RAINFALL ins.	0.5	0	0	0	0	0	0	0	0	0.5	0	0.5
RAINFALL mm	10	8	7	5	5	4	5	6	9	10	9	10
Days of Rainfall	2	1	1	1	1	1	1	1	2	2	2	2

Above: *The double-banded sandgrouse is a resident species of the Kalahari woodland and savanna.*
Right: *Four-wheel-drive tracks cut into the red sandveld of the Kalahari. This arid region supports a surprising variety of fauna, from puff adders and scorpions to gemsbok, hartebeest and ostrich.*
Below: *The huge nest built by sociable weavers is a distinctive feature of the stark Kalahari landscape, as is the tall camelthorn tree.*

Gobabis, situated about 205km (127 miles) east of Windhoek, is the centre of a cattle ranching district.

A Rhenish mission station was established here in about 1855, and twice had to be abandoned because of hostilities between Khausas Khoikhoi, Damara and Herero. Dating back to the turbulent 19th century is the Lazarette, an old hospital. The building has been declared a national monument, and plans are afoot to establish a museum here. Close to the town is a cemetery where, as in Okahandja and Omaruru, the Herero gather annually to pay tribute to their ancestors buried there.

Buitepos, the Namibian-Botswana border post, is about 214km (133 miles) farther on. From there it is a 480km (298 miles) journey to Maun, the gateway to the famed Okavango Delta and Chobe National Park. Note that this section of the Trans-Kalahari Highway is only suitable for four-wheel-drive vehicles, and it is not advisable to tackle it on your own.

A distinctive feature of the Kalahari landscape is the enormous communal nests that sociable weavers build on telephone posts and in camelthorn trees. The huge dome structures are constructed with twigs and straw and are divided into numerous separate chambers. Pygmy falcons and the colourful rosy-faced lovebird sometimes share the nests, while the giant eagle owl may be seen perching on top.

Bird-watchers should also look out for scaly-feathered and red-headed finches, the chat flycatcher, and double-banded, Namaqua and Burchell's sandgrouse when passing through the Kalahari. In the south, Burchell's and glossy starlings, and the southern yellowbilled hornbill, are some of the residents of the dry riverine forests.

The Kalahari Gemsbok Park in South Africa is unfortunately only accessible via the Twee Rivieren Gate, and the best route is via Keetmanshoop and Aroab on the C16.

35
A
B
C
D
1
2
3
4
5
41
47
OTJIWARONGO
WINDHOEK
MARIENTAL
OKAVANGO DELTA
Hereroland
Otjozondjou
Eiseb
Rooiboklaagte
Epukiro
Okarukurume
Otjinene
Otjinoko
Otjiyarwa
Dis Al
Summerdown
Okozondara
Okavarumendu
Okovimburu
Okatuwo
Omawewozonyanda
Epukiro
Rietfontein
Omur
Omaheke
Rietfontein
Drimiopsis
Xanagas
Tsootsha
Buitepos
Mamuno
Witvlei
Ninette
Gobabis
1530m
Babi-Babi
Okwa
Kalahari
BOTSWANA
Wit-Nossob
Swart-Nossob
Hoaseb Store
Gross Ums
Kule
Ncojane
Leonardville
TROPIC OF CAPRICORN
Ukwi Pan
Aminuis
Nossob
Vogelweide
Aranos
Stampriet
Olifants
Auob
Akanous
Lehututu
Hukuntsi
Lokgwabe
Gemsbok National Park
B6
C29
C22
C30
C20
C40
C23
C42
C39
C15
47
56
49
97
127
40
52
46
160
67
38
20
70
30
85
75
73
6
125
90
110
200
10

Diamond Coast and Namib Desert

The diamond-rich area surrounding the Lüderitz Peninsula (see page 18) on the wild and desolate Diamond Coast is controlled by Consolidated Diamond Mines, and is called the Sperrgebiet or 'forbidden territory'. Visitors may not leave the road or alight from their vehicles en route to Lüderitz, and a permit is required to visit the ghost towns that are of interest in the region. If you are travelling from Maltahöhe in the north, a detour to see the beautifully restored Duwisib Castle is recommended, while a stop at the small town of Bethanie, off the B4, will interest history enthusiasts. Several guest farms in the Maltahöhe area offer scenic surroundings and a variety of activities.

Look out for wild horses along the road to Lüderitz. No one is quite sure of their origins, but they are the only desert-dwelling feral horses in the world. The only water available for these animals is at Garub, and a viewing platform here gives visitors the opportunity to get a closer look at them.

The desert sands are reclaiming the once bustling mining town of Kolmanskop, while at Elizabeth Bay winds, mist and chemical weathering have eaten at the abandoned buildings. A permit is needed to visit the ghost town of Kolmanskop, where a guide will show you around the deserted mine and the remains of the once splendid houses. Police clearance is required to join a guided tour of skeletal, desolate Elizabeth Bay as mining operations have been resumed here.

Kolmanskop Tour Company will also take visitors with the necessary police clearance on an excursion to Atlas Bay seal colony, Pomona ghost town and Bogenfels rock arch. The latter curves 30m (98ft) above the waves and is a prominent feature of this lonely coastline, which is often wreathed in mist.

LÜDERITZ BAY	J	F	M	A	M	J	J	A	S	O	N	D
AVERAGE TEMP. °F	64	64	64	63	61	59	57	57	57	59	61	63
AVERAGE TEMP. °C	18	18	18	17	16	15	14	14	14	15	16	17
Hours of Sun Daily	7	6	7	7	8	8	8	7	6	7	7	7
SEA TEMP. °F	68	66	64	63	63	59	59	59	59	59	61	61
SEA TEMP. °C	20	19	18	17	17	15	15	15	15	15	16	16
RAINFALL ins.	0	0	0	0	0	0	0	0	0	0	0	0
RAINFALL mm	1	1	2	2	2	3	2	2	1	1	1	1
Days of Rainfall	1	1	1	1	1	1	0	1	1	0	1	0

Duwisib Castle, 70km (43 miles) south of Maltahöhe, is a wonderful example of a colonial turn-of-the-century mansion. The fortress-like building was designed for the German Baron von Wolf by Wilhelm Sander, who was also responsible for Fort Namutoni (*see* page 11). The original furniture and artworks were shipped from Germany to Lüderitz and then transported to Duwisib by oxwagon.

The London Missionary Society established a station to serve the Nama at Bethanie in 1814. The stone walls of Schmelen House (now a museum) date back to that period, while the Rhenish Mission Church was inaugurated in 1899. The original limestone church was used as a school until the 1970s, when it was abandoned to fall into disrepair. Also of interest is the Joseph Fredericks House (1883), used as a dwelling and council chamber by the Nama chief.

Top: *The once flourishing town of Kolmanskop boasted an ice-making factory, shops, school, casino and skittle alley, and elaborate two-storey mansions for the mine manager and engineer.*
Left: *Bogenfels rock arch on the Diamond Coast dwarfs the crashing waves below.*
Above: *The 22-room sandstone Duwisib Castle, restored in 1991, is a German-style fortress incongruously placed in a desolate desert landscape.*

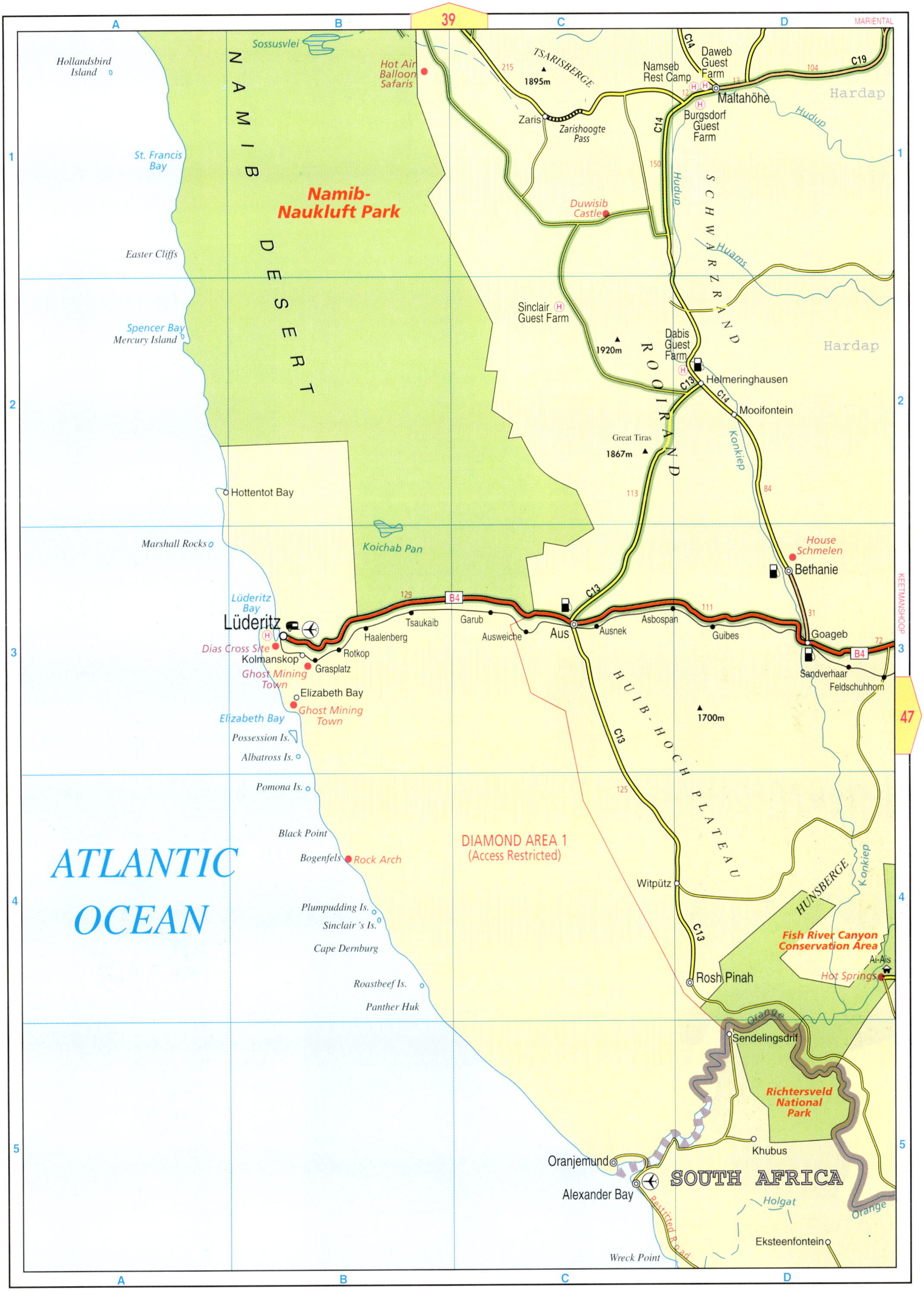
39
47
MARIENTAL
KEETMANSHOOP
NAMIB DESERT
Namib-Naukluft Park
Sossusvlei
Hot Air Balloon Safaris
Hollandsbird Island
St. Francis Bay
Easter Cliffs
Spencer Bay
Mercury Island
Hottentot Bay
Marshall Rocks
Koichab Pan
Lüderitz Bay
Lüderitz
Dias Cross Site
Kolmanskop
Ghost Mining Town
Grasplatz
Rotkop
Haalenberg
Tsaukaib
Garub
Ausweiche
Aus
Ausnek
Asbospan
Guibes
Goageb
Bethanie
House Schmelen
Sandverhaar
Feldschuhhorn
Elizabeth Bay
Ghost Mining Town
Possession Is.
Albatross Is.
Pomona Is.
Black Point
Bogenfels
Rock Arch
Plumpudding Is.
Sinclair 's Is.
Cape Dernburg
Roastbeef Is.
Panther Huk
ATLANTIC OCEAN
DIAMOND AREA 1
(Access Restricted)
TSARISBERGE
1895m
Zaris
Zarishoogte Pass
Namseb Rest Camp
Daweb Guest Farm
Maltahöhe
Burgsdorf Guest Farm
Hardap
Hudup
Duwisib Castle
SCHWARZRAND
Huams
Sinclair Guest Farm
1920m
Dabis Guest Farm
Helmeringhausen
Mooifontein
ROOIRAND
Great Tiras
1867m
Konkiep
HUIB-HOCH PLATEAU
1700m
Witpütz
HUNSBERGE
Fish River Canyon Conservation Area
Ai-Ais
Hot Springs
Rosh Pinah
Sendelingsdrif
Orange
Richtersveld National Park
Khubus
Oranjemund
Alexander Bay
SOUTH AFRICA
Holgat
Eksteenfontein
Wreck Point
Restricted Road
B4
C13
C14
C19
A
B
C
D
1
2
3
4
5

Southern Hinterland

The road leading to the Namibian-South African border post at Noordoewer via Keetmanshoop (see page 16) passes through a vast, mostly arid region that features striking geological formations, the most notable being the Fish River Canyon (see page 14), and a unique and intriguing plant life such as the tall quiver tree. Noordoewer is the starting point for exciting canoeing and rafting trips on the mighty Orange River. Summer days can be unbearably hot in this region, with recorded highs of over 45°C (113°F). Although winters are generally pleasant, it can be as cold as 4°C (39°F) in the evening and early morning.

Mukurob was one of Namibia's major attractions until some time during the night on 7 December 1988 when the 34m (111.5ft) sandstone column collapsed. Part of the narrow mudstone neck is still standing, but the sandstone head (estimated to have weighed about 637 tonnes) that it supported now lies in pieces around the base.

To the southwest is Brukkaros, an extinct volcano that rises 650m (2142ft) above the landscape. The floor of the crater lies about 350m (1148ft) below the rim and is 3km (2 miles) in diameter. Set aside a day to climb the slope and cross the crater to scale the western edge. The marvellous view of the surrounding countryside from there is ample reward for the strenuous hike.

The drought-resistant quiver tree, or *kokerboom*, is actually a tree aloe, and usually grows singly. However, near Keetmanshoop, about 250 impressive specimens that are estimated to be between 200 and 300 years old form the Quiver Tree Forest. They sport bright yellow flowers in around June and July, and the nectar attracts birds, insects and baboons. Giant's Playground, a fine example of the boulder-strewn landscape of the *Vratteveld* (*see* page 16), is close by. Both attractions are at their most picturesque in the early morning or later afternoon.

The Fish River Canyon Conservation Area (*see* page 14) is separated from the Richtersveld National Park in South Africa by the great Orange River. Desolate and inaccessible, this region of the border is best explored on a leisurely four- to six-day rafting or canoeing expedition downstream. A few white-water rapids en route add excitement to the journey. Nights are spent camping under the stars on the riverbank, and the trip can be combined with a five-day horseback trail.

Look out for some of Namibia's rare and protected plant species, such as the elephant's trunk, which at a distance looks somewhat like a person. A wide variety of succulents called stone plants or *Lithops* are also of interest in this winter-rainfall area.

KEETMANSHOOP	J	F	M	A	M	J	J	A	S	O	N	D
AVERAGE TEMP. °F	81	79	77	70	63	57	57	59	66	72	75	79
AVERAGE TEMP. °C	27	26	25	21	17	14	14	15	19	22	24	26
Hours of Sun Daily	12	10	10	10	10	9	10	10	10	11	11	12
RAINFALL ins.	1	1.5	1.5	0.5	0	0	0	0	0	0	0.5	0.5
RAINFALL mm	25	43	41	16	4	2	1	1	2	6	11	14
Days of Rainfall	11	11	11	5	2	1	1	0	1	3	5	7

Top: *The rim-shaped Brukkaros, an extinct volcano, dominates the surrounding countryside.*
Above: *Gemsbok gallop alongside the Orange River near Oranjemund, 5km (8 miles) from the river mouth. The long, straight horns and black-and-white facial markings of the desert-adapted gemsbok set it apart from other antelope species.*
Left: *Brightly coloured canoes beached for the night on the banks of the Orange River.*

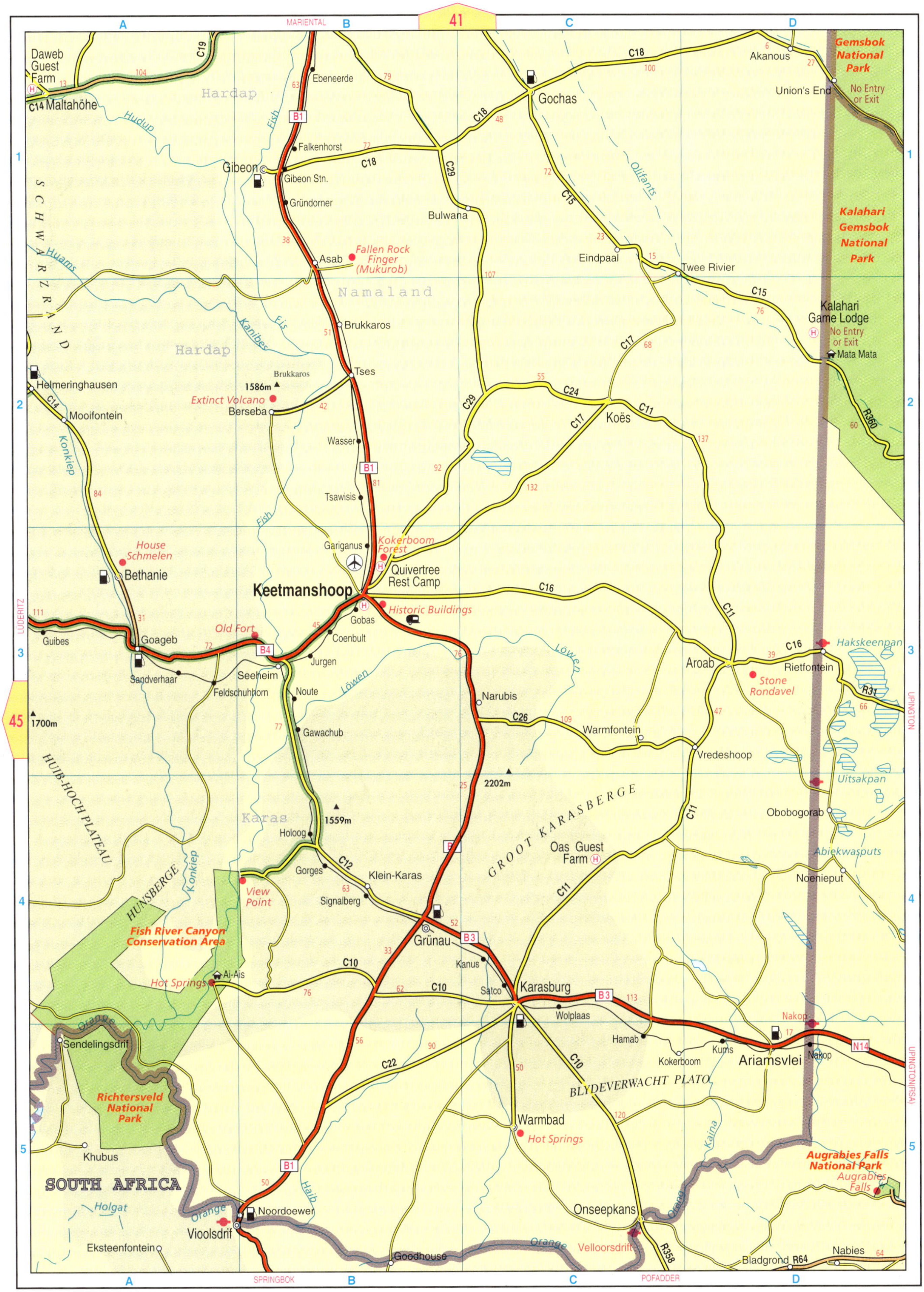
41
45
MARIENTAL
SPRINGBOK
POFADDER
LÜDERITZ
UPINGTON
UPINGTON(RSA)
Daweb Guest Farm
Maltahöhe
Hardap
Hudup
Fish
Ebeneerde
Falkenhorst
Gibeon
Gibeon Stn.
Gründorner
Gochas
Akanous
Union's End
Gemsbok National Park
No Entry or Exit
Bulwana
Olifants
Eindpaal
Twee Rivier
Kalahari Gemsbok National Park
Kalahari Game Lodge
Mata Mata
SCHWARZRAND
Huams
Asab
Fallen Rock Finger (Mukurob)
Namaland
Brukkaros
Kanibes
Fis
Tses
Helmeringhausen
Brukkaros 1586m
Extinct Volcano
Berseba
Mooifontein
Konkiep
Koës
Wasser
Tsawisis
Gariganus
Kokerboom Forest
Quivertree Rest Camp
House Schmelen
Bethanie
Keetmanshoop
Historic Buildings
Gobas
Coenbult
Old Fort
Guibes
Goageb
Sandverhaar
Feldschuhhorn
Seeheim
Jurgen
Noute
Löwen
Narubis
Warmfontein
Aroab
Stone Rondavel
Rietfontein
Hakskeenpan
Vredeshoop
Gawachub
1700m
2202m
HUIB-HOCH PLATEAU
Karas
1559m
Holoog
Uitsakpan
Obobogorab
GROOT KARASBERGE
Oas Guest Farm
Abiekwasputs
Noenieput
Gorges
Klein-Karas
Signalberg
HUNSBERGE
View Point
Fish River Canyon Conservation Area
Grünau
Kanus
Satco
Karasburg
Ai-Ais
Hot Springs
Orange
Sendelingsdrif
Wolplaas
Hamab
Kokerboom
Kums
Nakop
Ariamsvlei
Richtersveld National Park
BLYDEVERWACHT PLATO
Warmbad
Hot Springs
Khubus
Kaina
SOUTH AFRICA
Holgat
Haib
Noordoewer
Vioolsdrif
Eksteenfontein
Goodhouse
Onseepkans
Velloorsdrif
Augrabies Falls National Park
Augrabies Falls
Bladgrond
Nabies
B1
B3
B4
C10
C11
C12
C13
C14
C15
C16
C17
C18
C19
C22
C24
C26
C29
R31
R358
R360
N14
R64

Index